Praise for *Stories of the Generous Life*

"Our generosity stories are powerful examples of Scripture lived out ... and they are attractive to a watching world. Bill High is a catalyst among countless givers who are living out their generosity stories in powerful ways. His insights into their lives as described in this book are priceless. I believe this will help you, and the people you lead, create your own generosity stories that can change the world."

—Patrick Johnson
Founder
GenerousChurch

"One of the most powerful tools God uses to encourage us is the example of others. If you want motivation to live all out for Jesus, then read this book! It is full of challenging stories from people who had one thing in common—they were willing to give God everything. Then, they got to watch God do miracles as He multiplied what they put in His hands."

—Mike Bickley
Lead Pastor
Olathe Bible Church

"Aside from the inspired Scriptures, nothing has catalyzed my giving journey more than stories of other givers. *Stories of the Generous Life* will strengthen your faith, empower you to step into new giving experiences, and encourage your walk with the Lord."

—Jeff Anderson
Founder
Acceptable Gift

"In this transformational book, Bill High gives us stories of generous Christ followers that will challenge the way we steward financial resources. In this easy to read book, you will find every story is a living, tangible picture of Kingdom-of-God generosity.

Jesus related to everyday people by teaching through stories. And, using stories, Bill High teaches us that generosity loosens shackles and frees prisoners from the chains of egocentric living. This book provides the reader with a number of pictures of radical individuals who took practical steps of faith. You will be inspired, motivated, and challenged to do likewise."

—**Jimmy Dodd**
President and Founder
PastorServe

"As someone who has watched lives changed as people become givers, I appreciate how Bill High captured the principle that generosity is not about the size of your bank account, but is truly about your commitment to be the heart and hands of Christ. Everyone benefits as we live the generous life. Thanks for this reminder!"

—**Howard Boyd**
NCF / Generosity Council
(Branson, Missouri)

"You will be inspired in reading these stories of generosity. It is a great reminder that our stuff is a spiritual matter and God will reward our generous use of it."

—**Vernon Armitage**
Ministry Pastor
Willow Creek Association

"Jesus said much would be expected from those to whom much had been entrusted. This can feel threatening until you recognize God's plan for His stuff is SO much more fun than your plan for His stuff! Bill High provides real stories of people who know the joy of a generous life. This book is nothing short of compelling.

It will help you discover what your heart has always longed for as you find it begins and ends with a generous life."

—Jim West
Lead Pastor
Colonial Presbyterian Church

"I highly recommend *Stories of a Generous Life*. When I started reading, I couldn't stop. I was inspired, challenged, and convicted. Bill High writes in a way that is conversational in nature, as if he were sitting across the table telling the story. After you read one story, you'll want to read them all."

—Gary Kendall
Lead Pastor
Indian Creek Community Church

STORIES OF THE
Generous Life

STORIES OF THE
Generous Life

ORDINARY PEOPLE. EXTRAORDINARY GENEROSITY.

WILLIAM F. HIGH
WITH MISSY CALVERT

WinePressPublishing
Great Books, Defined.

WinePress Publishing is honored to present this title in partnership with the author. The views expressed or implied in this work are those of the author. WinePress provides our imprint seal representing design excellence, creative content and high quality production. To learn more about Responsible Publishing™ visit www.winepresspublishing.com.

The author of this book has waived a portion of the publisher's recommended professional editing services. As such, any related errors found in this finished product are not the responsibility of the publisher.

Unless otherwise noted, all Scriptures are taken from *The Holy Bible: English Standard Version*, copyright © 2001, Wheaton: Good News Publishers. Used by permission. All rights reserved.

Scripture marked MSG are taken from *The Message*. Copyright © 1993, 1994, 1995, 1996, 2000, 2001, 2002. Used by permission of NavPress Publishing Group.

ISBN 13: 978-1-60615-249-2
ISBN 10: 1-60615-249-1
Library of Congress Catalog Card Number: 2013906321

This book is dedicated to my mother, Kimi High. She has been a model of generosity her entire life. While she never possessed much in financial resources, she gave us perseverance, continuity, time, and love. I'm most grateful.

Contents

Foreword

THE POWER OF Story. We love that idea.

Serving at the National Christian Foundation (NCF) has given us the privilege of coming alongside hundreds of families in their giving journeys. Among these families are countless stories of people on a journey of generosity—an adventure inspired by the Spirit of God as He gets hold of their hearts and they begin to dream big with their giving.

These are the kind of stories you are about to experience in this book. Although very different, at the center of every one of them you will catch a glimpse of the greatest story ever told ... of a Savior who gave all because He loves us. And you'll learn how all of these givers have responded to the redemption story in their own unique ways with ever-increasing generosity.

In our work, we have observed that generous people are the most joyful because they know true freedom. So why aren't Christians talking more about generosity? There is much discussion about prayer, Scripture, evangelism, and fellowship, but we tend to avoid the subject of giving and generosity.

However, there's never been a better time to expand the conversation. We are at one of the critical turning points in all of history. A recent survey by Boston College Center of Wealth and Philanthropy reports that trillions of dollars will be transferred to subsequent generations by the year 2052. With this great wealth transfer, we need to educate people on how to wisely transfer that wealth to Kingdom causes instead of letting that wealth dissipate, as so often occurs.

That is why we are so grateful for this book and for the givers who have shared their stories here. And we appreciate the work of leaders like Bill High and other NCF team members around the country who are engaged in this great work of serving givers and engaging with their stories.

It is our sincere hope that the generosity in these stories will inspire your own big dreams to influence those around the corner ... or around the world. As you connect with the challenges and hopes in these pages, we pray your faith will grow and you will see a bigger picture of the story God is writing in your own life.

We encourage you to read this book, think on it, and act on it. You may even want to share these stories with your church, small group, ministry you support, or with your friends. Even better, add the power of your story to the conversation and share your own journey of generosity. You never know who might be inspired ... maybe even you!

Bill Williams
Chief Executive Officer
National Christian
Foundation

David Wills
President
National Christian
Foundation

Preface

I LOVE STORY. I came to Christ because of a children's Bible storybook. When we hear, read, or see someone's story, we inevitably see a picture of ourselves. We learn, and we change. That's why Jesus told stories.

This book contains stories of people—real people—on the road to the generous life. Not one of them would say they have arrived.

As you read you'll note that we included a variety of stories. Not all the stories are about giving money. Some people gave cars, real estate, businesses, careers, or their time. Some of the people are not wealthy—at least, not by the American standard. Some of the people are young. Some are senior citizens. Within these stories, I think you'll find at least one to be similar to your story.

At the end of each story, you'll find a few questions to stimulate your own journey. Take your time. It's also designed for you to read easily—all at once or in multiple sessions. We've kept it short intentionally.

As followers of Christ, we are called to live a freely generous life. God uses generosity as a catalyst for healing, an agent of change, and a builder of faith. Even the smallest gifts have the power to affect eternity and radically transform people's lives. In His Word, God tells us to store up treasure where moth and rust cannot destroy and where thieves cannot break in and steal.

Generosity is a lifestyle of giving your resources, your expertise, and your love to influence eternity. We may recognize this call to give, but in the chaos of the everyday, we are tempted to accumulate stuff and hold on to our lives just as they are. We often lose sight of the generous life, and we can't imagine giving our money or our time without calculating what it may cost us.

However, if you desire to leave a legacy for the next generation and to see people's lives transformed during your lifetime, if you want your business and your ministry to count for all eternity, take a risk and plunge into the generous life. Just be prepared, this journey will change you as you discover true life is found when you give yours away.

William F. High
Chief Executive Officer
National Christian Foundation *Heartland*

> *Whoever loves his life loses it, and whoever hates his life in this world will keep it for eternal life.* (John 12:25)

Acknowledgments

THIS BOOK WOULD not have been written without the contributions and support of the following people. Thank you for your faithful service.

My wife, Brooke, continues to be my best friend and confidant. My four children: Ashley, Jessica, Nathan, and Joseph have also participated with me in this journey. Ashley edited the book and Jessica took the photographs.

Missy Calvert interviewed all the people in the book and captured their stories beautifully. Aspen Emmett McCarthy (Andy's Photography by Aspen) took the photo of LeahBelle's hill, and her kindness was greatly appreciated. Katie Krueger served as the final editor for the manuscript. Adam Cothes, Mike Owens, and the team at WinePress Publishing offered high-quality service and support.

Finally, my colleagues and board members at the National Christian Foundation: I've had the privilege to intersect with your stories, and you are all stories of the generous life.

CHAPTER ONE

Holding Orphans with Jesus' Arms

Mike & Beth Fox

BETH WILL TELL you it's not safe. Engaging in the lives of orphans is a dangerous and painful undertaking for hearts; it will change you. Mike and Beth Fox, founders of the Global Orphan Project, never intended to start a nonprofit, but they also never anticipated the joy of sharing Christ's love with orphans. As God transformed their hearts, they began a journey they never could have imagined.

In 1991, Mike Fox was successful in the world's eyes—he was a brilliant salesman who had just begun his own business. But inside, Mike was miserable, wrestling with a crumbling family, a struggling business, and a selfish lifestyle. Eventually, his business failed.

"A lot of things weren't going the way I had it planned," Mike said. "It was a point of surrender. I had tried everything my way."

In 1993, Mike, who was then in his mid-thirties, married Beth. Two years later, he surrendered his life to Christ, but it was still several years before Christ penetrated his heart in a real and unshakable way. Within the next ten years, the Lord turned Mike's life around, blessing him with success in the propane gas business.

Beth had been a believer from a young age, but a brain aneurism forced her to lean on God as never before. She recovered, and Christ once again became the focus of her life. God continued to bless Mike and Beth financially; however, generosity was not yet on their radar.

"We weren't very giving people," Mike said. "We did what most Americans do. We gave out of our surplus, but we weren't going to miss going to dinner or buying the next car."

A Change of Heart

One day, Mike and Beth were asked to get involved in the lives of orphans by sponsoring an orphanage in Thailand. Mike agreed and wrote a check for $750 to house seventeen children. Curious, Mike traveled to Thailand to see the effect of his gift. What he found changed his life. The money had been stretched to house nineteen of the most grateful and generous kids Mike had ever met.

"Mike came back a changed man after spending time with those children," Beth recalled. "I knew, and we knew, without a shadow of a doubt that God had a hold of our hearts. He had big plans for our future, and it wasn't going to be what we planned."

Mike and Beth couldn't shake this new passion to help more children. After Beth's first trip to Haiti, orphans captured her heart as well. "I held a little baby on my lap and realized a dollar in the United States can make a huge difference in this child's life," Beth said. "That trip was a turning point for me to really join hands with Mike and say, 'I'm all in.' "

The Foxes couldn't stop talking about their experiences to friends, family, and anyone who would listen. They looked for more opportunities to obey God, thinking they could fund five or ten more homes for orphans. "In the process of doing that, this entire ministry kind of got its own set of wheels and got some momentum," Mike said.

Using their backgrounds in business, the Foxes began implementing organizational systems and hiring employees. Eventually, their passion became its own entity, and in 2004, the Foxes founded the Global Orphan Project, Inc. (originally known as C3 Missions International). The next year, in 2005, Mike officially left the corporate world.

"We kept saying yes to Christ, and He kept opening doors," Beth said. "This is not our plan; it's all God's plan."

Down the road, God led the Foxes to walk through yet another door in obedience. In 2009, God asked them to release the Global Orphan Project, or GO Project, allowing it to be championed by other passionate individuals. Today, it is run by hundreds of GO Project advocates.

"It was kind of hard, honestly, because then you're not in control. We have since learned that it was probably the very best thing we did for these children," Mike said. "Every day someone else will hear, get involved, or go that we have never met or may never meet."

Only Hope

After the devastating Haitian earthquake of 2010, Beth met a thirteen-year-old girl alone on the streets of Haiti. Orphaned and impregnated by rape, the girl was broken and hopeless, unable to look Beth in the eyes.

"God put me in that specific place at that specific time to love her," Beth said. "I almost felt like, for the first time in my life, I was Jesus' arms. I could make a difference in that child's life that no one else could because she was looking to me as a female figure in her life to get her through this."

> "I almost felt like, for the first time in my life, I was Jesus' arms."

Through Beth's love, this girl learned about Christ's love. She now has hope. She lives in a GO Project home near a local church where she goes to school, works in a sewing center, and has the assurance of food and safety for her healthy baby girl.

Today, the GO Project seeks to help other children like her, the most vulnerable orphans in many of the world's poorest countries, aiming to provide security and hope in the bleakest of circumstances. The ministry empowers local churches to create a village system that includes children's homes with mommas to care for them, a school, and infrastructure like kitchens, latrines, and wells. Their hope is that the children will praise God, not donors, for what they have received.

"We understand hunger, we understand poverty, we understand no clean water, we understand lack of education or school uniforms, but at the end of the day, our mantra, our desire, our passion is for these kids to know Christ," Mike said. "The sooner the better, the more the better. It just seems like we can't do it fast enough."

100 Percent Commitment

Mike and Beth, along with other private donors, cover the entire overhead costs for the ministry, which allows GO Project to commit 100 percent of donations to orphan care.

"I just know how I am," Mike said. "If I thought part of my donation was going to pay the light bill, I would wonder, why do they have the thermostat turned on? How much are they spending on air travel? How much do these people get paid? By removing all of that, we have literally removed about 99 percent of the barriers of entry. That's why most people don't give, because they think it's not going to be used wisely or it's not going to be used for the cause they have been told. We believe that this will make more money available for His Kingdom. And it has."

This strategy has released a flood of unity between staff, churches, and volunteers, who take ownership in the ministry. "There are thousands of people, and they do not say, 'Here's what *they* do at the Global Orphan Project.' They say, 'Here's what *we* do.' 'Here's what *I* do.' It has transformed so many hearts," said Joe Knittig, CEO of the Global Orphan Project.

By paying for the ministry's expenses, Joe believes donors can demystify the giving process for others and unleash the power of financial transparency.

"It is one of the shrewdest and wisest ways I've seen generosity used in the ministry world, and it is big in this ministry," he said.

Unsafe Territory

GO Project helps the orphans who are the poorest of the poor, left on the streets to fend for themselves. "If they don't find a place to either beg or steal or get into a dumpster that day, they will not eat," Mike said. The Foxes, along with GO Project staff and partners, bathe the ministry in prayer, refusing to give up on these kids who have no one to speak for them.

But there are dark days in the ministry's sacred fight for orphans. "I believe the evil one so wants nobody to get into the hearts of these kids that he will do everything within his deceptive power to destroy that entity," Mike said. "Our job is to stay pure, to stay humble, and to be tough in the fight. The first time we quit fighting, these kids will perish."

Mike and Beth have seen many lives unexpectedly changed because of their involvement with these children. They describe the ministry as two-fold, affecting orphans and donors alike.

"These kids are the most loving, caring children," Beth said. "They are focused on Christ and on life and on all the things they are so thankful for, even though they have so little."

These children have taught the Foxes much about generosity. "We think they still don't have much because they don't have all the stuff we have," Mike said. "They don't think like that. When we spend time with these children, they will literally give us anything they have, which may be nothing more than their clothes."

Although God has led Mike and Beth to be financially generous to this cause, they have learned it is not about the money. "It's not really your dollar;

> "You can surrender all your money, but that's not really what God wants."

it's your heart," Beth said. "You can surrender all your money, but that's not really what God wants. He has all the money in the world. It's your own personal heart He wants you to surrender and give to Him."

It's a battleground; it's unsafe territory, but it is a fight for the lives and hearts of God's children. God has transformed Mike and

Beth through this unexpected journey, and although they don't know where it will lead them tomorrow, they are willing to be the arms of Jesus to orphans, to be the love of Christ to the ones the world has forgotten.

Your Story:

1. Like Beth says, getting involved in people's lives is unsafe. It's difficult and painful to see the messiness of broken lives. Are you willing to risk your heart to love the unlovable? How are you being the arms of Jesus to people around you?

2. Do you share Mike and Beth's passion for orphans? Read these verses and reflect on God's heart for the fatherless: James 1:27, Isaiah 1:17, and Matthew 25:45.

3. Mike and Beth have seen that paying for GO Project's overhead has freed other people to give generously. How can you adjust your giving to remove barriers for other people?

View of LeahBelle's hill from her porch

CHAPTER TWO

Giving Away the Hill Land

LeahBelle Neil

LEAHBELLE SAT ON her porch one summer night, enjoying the clean Colorado air. The moon shone gently, illuminating her land in the distance.

"The question came to mind, *Why are you keeping that hill?* I answered right away, *I don't want anyone up there*," LeahBelle recalled. "This impression came again, *Is that a good reason?* At that point I knew: I was hearing from the Lord."

After the death of her first husband, LeahBelle inherited 320 acres of land, 160 of which were the hill. "The land wasn't being used. It was lying idle, but I didn't want anybody up there," she said. "That's poor stewardship, but I didn't know what to do with it."

Letting Go

LeahBelle considered deeding the land to charity in her will, but she felt God calling her to use it during her lifetime. She struggled to let God have it.

"I didn't want to let the hill go because I cherish our privacy and the quietness where we live," she said.

The Lord kept gently pressing LeahBelle that night as she sat on her porch.

"That is one of the clearest experiences of my life. The Lord was speaking to me and letting me know it was Him," she said. "So I said, 'Well, I don't know what to do with it.' I assumed I would get all the information I needed about getting help, but the conversation was over. I said, 'Come on, Lord, what do You want me to do?' "

A few months later, God responded when she received a visit from two Christian men who often hunted on her land.

"One of them said to me, 'LeahBelle, why don't you put that hill in a charitable trust?' I said, 'I don't know how.'"

The man said he would send a lawyer to help her. They eventually contacted a lawyer with the National Christian Foundation. Soon, LeahBelle was working on a plan to give away her land to benefit God's Kingdom. In a matter of months, LeahBelle had transferred her land into a charitable trust.

"I would have sold that whole hill for four or five thousand dollars," she said, "But it was appraised for about $348,000."

The Gift of Giving

LeahBelle was born in 1924 and grew up on a family farm during the Great Depression.

"We did well to keep our heads above water," she said. "The family was self-sufficient, but we had to work hard to meet our own needs."

When she was thirteen, LeahBelle attended a Christian summer camp simply to escape work. The last night of the camp, she understood the message of Jesus for the first time. "That night, I wanted to have Jesus come into my heart, but I was frozen to the spot," she said. "There was a spiritual battle going on."

However, LeahBelle eventually mustered up the courage to move. "I finally was able to make that first step, and I just about trampled the girl in front of me after I got moving," she said. "I was saved from the top of my head to the bottom of my feet, and I've never doubted it for seventy-three years."

Though LeahBelle had undeniably found Jesus, she was young in her faith. She married a church-attending, but unsaved, man named Oscar.

"It took me twenty years, in my ignorance, to figure out that man was lost. He was very churchy, but he did not know he wasn't saved either."

When Oscar was diagnosed with cancer of the esophagus, LeahBelle continued to pray for his salvation. Two years before he passed away, Oscar gave his life to Christ.

"He made a profession of faith, and he is waiting for me in glory!"

When she became a believer, LeahBelle said the Lord gave her the gift of giving—something she discovered fully as she was mentored in her mid-thirties. "That is how I learned to give; God put it in my heart," she said.

Touching the World from Colorado

Giving away her land provided LeahBelle with many opportunities to be generous. LeahBelle and her second husband, Joe, give away at least half of their income each year.

"We have all we need. God has supplied all of our needs according to His riches and glory," she said. "I am so glad to have income to pass along now instead of waiting until I die."

> "I am so glad I have income to pass along now instead of waiting until I die."

LeahBelle and Joe have supported missionaries in Greece, Kenya, Utah, and East Asia. LeahBelle knows every missionary she supports personally. Some have stayed in her home, and she has visited her friends in Utah and Greece.

"It's not my money; it's God's money, and I just want to distribute it as He leads me, but I don't just randomly give it away," she said. "I want [to] know where it is going and what it is doing."

LeahBelle still looks up at that hill from her porch. She gives God all the glory for helping her let it go so the land can be used for His Kingdom. Now LeahBelle says, "When I look up at the hill, I see people from every tribe and nation who will be reached for the gospel of Christ. That's a good trade ... land for people. I know it was God who did the whole thing. I just stand in awe. I take no credit—God did it all."

"That's a good trade—land for people."

After a brief illness, LeahBelle entered into glory on March 2, 2013.

Your Story:

1. Like LeahBelle, what "hill" is God asking you to release for His glory? Remember that it is not about a dollar amount—it is God seeking your heart.

2. What is holding you back? Have an honest conversation with God; ask Him to give you a heart for His Kingdom above your own comfort.

3. Starting is often the hardest part. What information or resources do you need to move forward? Write down three practical steps you can take toward good stewardship:

   1. _____

   2. _____

   3. _____

Building a Purpose-Driven Company

Pat & Beth McCown

WHEN PAT MCCOWN and his business partner, Brett Gordon, put together what they thought was a reasonable business plan in 1999, they had little idea where God would take their construction company.

"It was in our hearts to put together a different kind of construction company—one that was built on core values of integrity, performance, and relationships," Pat said. "By God's grace, the company has grown to be one of the largest construction companies in Kansas City."

The success of McCownGordon Construction has opened up doors for Pat and his wife, Beth, to give from the company's profits, live generously in their personal lives, and be one of God's lights to Kansas City.

"All of this resulted from having a mindset that is not necessarily profit-driven, but being a part of something that is bigger and more important than simply making another buck," Pat said.

A Larger Purpose

A year and a half from its inception, McCownGordon was recognized as the second fastest growing, privately owned business in

America by *Entrepreneur* magazine. The following year, the company was ranked the fourth fastest-growing new business.

"You can't write a business plan like that, you can't work that hard, or even that smart. It's only by the sovereign will of God that this could ever happen," Beth said.

Early in the operation of McCownGordon, Pat and Brett made an unusual business decision. They committed to give 10 percent of the company's annual profits to the community.

"When you boil it all down, it's very simple; God extended His grace and His mercy toward us at McCownGordon for a purpose larger than simply making money," Pat said. "Our company is more defined as a purpose-driven company than a profit-driven company."

The company gives to faith-based organizations as well as community causes like the Juvenile Diabetes Research Foundation, the Ronald McDonald House, and Children's Mercy Hospital. McCownGordon has exceeded 10 percent most years, giving away an average of 15 percent of profits over the last seven years.

"God has chosen to bless our company, and we take it very seriously," Beth said. "We recognize His provision and His free will over our company. He can do with it as He will. Hopefully we will be wise stewards with what He has given us for this season."

> "God has chosen to bless our company and we take it very seriously."

Learning Stewardship

The McCowns believe God has allowed them to be profitable so they can invest more in the Kingdom. With that blessing comes the responsibility to discern when and where to give.

"Giving it all away may seem like a very noble thing to do, and maybe that is what the Lord would have for some," Pat said. "For us, we feel like He has given us financial resources, and He intends for us to grow and cultivate them even more."

Pat and Beth also have a commitment to generosity outside of their business, and the success of McCownGordon has led them to new ways of managing their giving.

"As more funds have come in, we have obviously had to take on the stewardship of those," Pat said. "Part of that was becoming involved with the National Christian Foundation and setting up a giving fund."

The couple decided to include their four children in the decision-making process for the family foundation. "That really unites us in many ways as a family," Pat said. "They get a chance to see firsthand what it feels like, what it means, and what effect even the simplest act of generosity has on other people and organizations."

One Christmas Eve, the McCowns' daughter presented the family with her colleague's story: a young nurse and mother of three suddenly lost her husband to a stroke and could not afford the funeral and burial. The McCown family decided to cover her expenses.

"Our daughter called this woman and put her on a conference call," Beth recalled. "We were all able to participate in the gift, which just blessed our family much more than we probably ever blessed her. We shared an incredible sense of awe, seasoned with joy, and we got to do it as a family."

Responding to His Call

The McCowns have tried to establish a biblical framework to direct their giving. "The poor, the orphans, the needy, the widowed, and the foreigners are the five things we see from Scripture that we need to be giving to beyond the tithe," Pat said.

"Thankfully, we are past the point of trying to be obedient with our teeth gritted," Beth said. "God has made us very happy and content with the generosity aspect of our lives. That is something that gives us great pleasure, and the more we learn to do it right, the more fun it all becomes."

For example, one day the Lord impressed upon Pat and Beth to give to their friends who were missionaries in Guatemala. Although they had not spoken with their friends in years, the McCowns donated online and then let them know the funds were on their way. Within hours, Pat and Beth received an e-mail from Guatemala. Joyfully, their friends explained how the gift had come at a very critical day for their ministry.

"They were thrilled," Beth said. "Of course, that brought us as much joy as it did them. You just smile and laugh when decisions work out like that." The McCowns saw the news as confirmation from the Lord. "Hearing God's direction for any aspect of your life—whether financial or otherwise—can be a challenge," Pat said. "Little tokens like that say this was right, we didn't miss God here, we actually heard the voice of the Lord."

A Light in Kansas City

As McCownGordon Construction has continued to grow, it has provided opportunities for Pat and Beth to lead and serve in their city. Beth served two years as chairwoman for a City Union Mission luncheon called "Women Who Change the Heart of the City," which honors influential women in Kansas City. Since then, Beth has continued to be involved with the event.

"This, and other platforms, would have not been available without McCownGordon," Beth said. "I have definitely seen specific lives changed through participation in the event, and I have seen City Union Mission grow as well. It's a great example of how generosity begets generosity."

Pat compares his position as CEO to a pastor in many ways. He and Beth agree that God has called them to teach and shepherd others. "It is not all about us and what God has given to us; we have a responsibility to help others move along in the path of living generously," Pat explained.

> "Pat compares his position as CEO to a pastor in many ways."

The McCowns have experienced God's blessings, and they are embracing the opportunity to live generously. "It's not about living large; it is about living in God's will," Beth said. "I do not want to stand before my Maker in heaven and say I used half of my surplus wisely. I want to be able to say I was as faithful as I could be with all the resources and blessings He gave us."

Your Story:

1. What is the purpose of your business or job? Ask God to show you how to use your company or career for more than profit.

2. Have you included your spouse and family in your giving? Set aside time for a family meeting. Discuss people, organizations, or issues that are close to your hearts and brainstorm ways you can live generously together.

3. The McCowns focus their giving on orphans, widows, foreigners, the poor, and the needy. Read Proverbs 19:17, James 1:27, Isaiah 58:6–11, and Deuteronomy 10:19. What other verses can you find about biblical giving?

CHAPTER FOUR

Scam Artist to Million-Dollar Miracle

Scott & Kirsten Lewis

A S A YOUNG boy, Scott Lewis had little material wealth and even less stability. His parents divorced when he was a toddler, which began a childhood of musical homes. He changed schools nine times before his high school graduation. His dad worked as a barber but often had to support his children by "borrowing" money Scott had saved by shoveling snow.

With all the change came a desire to fit in; Scott began drinking and doing drugs in his early teen years. At the same time, he pushed himself hard in school and sports, determined to create a better life.

"I knew the only way I was going to get out of my ghetto was to get a scholarship and go to college," Scott said. Scott excelled and achieved a high ACT score. He was eligible for a four-year college scholarship—he just needed his dad to fill out a financial aid form. That was the first time Scott saw his dad cry.

Scott's dad said, "Son, I can't fill this out. When you were a little boy, I had to make a decision between paying my taxes and feeding you. I didn't file that year, and they lost me in the system. I've never paid taxes. If I fill out this form, they'll catch me, and I'll go to prison." Scott's hope of college disappeared. He was crushed.

"I managed to scrape up a vocational scholarship for $600 and go to a little community college to learn how to pound nails in construction," Scott said. "I did that for a couple years and wallowed in a pity party. I started doing more drugs and drinking."

The Fast Lane

Unhappy and eager to get out of small-town Iowa, Scott dropped everything when he learned about an opportunity to make substantial money. He drove to Waco, Texas, with $60 in his pocket and joined a group of traveling "salesmen."

"One guy put me in his pickup truck and told me to shut up and watch him," Scott said. "Two days later he said, 'You think you can do this?' I said, 'Sure I can. You guys are just acting.'" For the next three-and-a-half years, Scott traveled the country performing sales scams.

"I became the number one guy in the United States out of five-hundred guys doing it," he said. "I used to fly all over the country just to train people how to scam."

Scott's success led him to the luxurious lifestyle he could have only imagined as a kid. "All my childhood dreams began to come true," he said. "By the time I was twenty-one I had three Corvettes, two big Chevy trucks, a camper, a jet boat, a house in Phoenix and a house up in Seattle, nice clothes, jewelry, and money in my pocket. I had all the drugs I wanted, and I lived a very, very fast lifestyle."

But God had big plans for this radical salesman. In 1983, Scott traveled to Sacramento, California, to visit a girl. To his surprise, this girl had recently become a Christian. She insisted that Scott talk to her stepbrother about Christ. Scott reluctantly agreed.

Though the conversation intrigued him, Scott wasn't ready to give up his lifestyle. Then the man presented him with a difficult question: Was he sure he would be alive tomorrow to make a decision for Christ?

Scott answered with a resounding, "No! I have had .357s in my face and .25s in my gut. I've done more LSD and cocaine than anyone should be able to get off the floor and walk away from. I have friends who are dead right now because of the life we are living."

Over the next few days, the truth of Christ and the gospel began to penetrate Scott's heart. "I began to realize, if these promises are true, this is what I've been looking for my whole life. I've been looking for someone who would love me and be a friend and never leave."

Scott returned to the guy who shared the gospel with him. He was ready to accept Christ. "It was like a thousand pounds came off me. For

> "If these promises are true, this is what I've been looking for my whole life."

the first time in my life, I was truly free. All those masks I had been wearing—I threw them all away. I flew back to Phoenix the next day, quit my job, and dumped my stuff. I had to get completely out of all of that."

The Christian Life

Scott started over in Sacramento, where he focused the passion he had for sales on God. "I was the most zealous, fired-up Christian you could find," he said.

For the next two and a half years, Scott was discipled by a pastor and got involved in a church. He met his wife, Kirsten, in Sunday school. After they were married, Scott opened his own tool business, and he and Kirsten continued to serve God together. "We were doing the Christian life as well as we thought we could," Scott said.

However, God was about to shake up Scott's life once again. Scott went to Mexico with a missions group to show *The Jesus Film*. He watched in amazement as more than 400 people came to see the movie and 180 made a decision for Christ. He felt compelled to get involved with the film.

So, when he and Kirsten were invited to attend the premiere in Albania, they decided to go. "It was not a convenient time for us to go to Albania for a couple of weeks," Scott recalled. "We had a toddler, and Kirsten was nursing our second child. But we got out the globe, sat down in the middle of the living room floor, and started spinning it, saying, 'Where in the world is Albania?'"

Six weeks later, they boarded a plane and left the country. They had the opportunity to share the gospel in a high school classroom in Albania, and almost every student accepted Christ. A young girl stopped Scott as he was leaving. She said, "Please, sir, don't waste time talking to people who don't want to know God. So many people want to know God."

No Wasted Time

Their experience in Albania and the words of that high school girl changed everything. Scott and Kirsten returned home ready to shut down their business and move to Albania for full-time missions.

"When you run a business, you spend a lot of time doing things that aren't spiritual in nature—paperwork, taxes, inventory," Scott said. "We wanted to get back and reach people for Christ."

Two weeks before they planned to close the business, God intervened. Scott woke up early one morning with an overwhelming sense of God's presence telling him not to go to Albania. Instead, God told Scott to stay in the United States and keep doing exactly what he had been doing.

Confused but obedient, Scott and Kirsten continued working. Two months later, they attended a Campus Crusade for Christ conference, where they heard from Dr. Bill Bright, the founder of Campus Crusade and producer of *The Jesus Film*. Dr. Bright challenged the audience to take the film to the nations. He was looking for twelve hundred people to each give $1 million to the cause.

Scott and Kirsten wanted to participate, so they approached Dr. Bright to ask how they could make that happen. Dr. Bright suggested they set a goal of giving $50,000 the next year and watch what God would do. Scott was bewildered. That was more than his business made the previous year, but he didn't want to argue with Dr. Bright. Scott returned to his company excited to tell his staff they were going to give away $50,000 for Christ. "I can't imagine what they were all thinking," he said.

Miracles in the Tool Business

Scott and Kirsten established a modest living and continued to work their business to reach their seemingly lofty goal. "We didn't already have a high net worth; we were just a couple of young kids eating what we needed and giving the rest away," Scott said. Near the end of the year, Scott's business had given about $20,000.

One day, Scott received an unexpected call from a man in Jupiter, Florida. "When you're in Sacramento, and you've got this little tool business, Jupiter may as well be Pluto," Scott laughed. The man was looking for a specific tool. Scott wasn't familiar with it, but he had seen one in an auction advertisement, so he took a risk. He attended the auction and found the tool. In the process, Scott met a second customer who asked him for something similar. Those two deals brought in $30,000—the remaining amount needed to meet their giving goal.

It seemed perfect, but Scott struggled to give it all away. How was he ever going to reach $1 million if he didn't build up his business? "I realized the devil was trying to get me to not do it. I called my secretary and said, 'Quick, write the check before I change my mind!'"

> "Quick, write the check before I change my mind!"

The following day, Scott's company was closed for inventory. After a half-day of work, they decided to open the store. "We turned the open sign around, we unlocked the doors, and we started answering the phone," Scott recalled. "We did $65,000 in sales that afternoon; $27,000 of that was profit. God gave almost all of it back in that one afternoon when we weren't even supposed to be working."

Scott later asked the man from Jupiter how he found him. The man said he had been attempting to contact a Scott's Machinery in Alabama. "That's when I knew God did a miracle," Scott said. "He provided what we couldn't provide."

Scott and Kirsten continued to work toward their million-dollar goal, giving away $100,000 the following year. Sometimes the company made overhead; other times they fell short, but Scott continued to trust God.

"It's Business 101—of course, I never went to college, so I never took it—but the first thing they would have told you is don't drain the corporate account. You have to have money to pay overhead," Scott said.

If Scott ever hesitated in giving, Kirsten was right there to encourage him. After seven faithful years, they completed their million-dollar commitment.

God's Story

Scott and Kirsten have seen God's provision, but their story is far from a fairy tale. They wrestled through years of financial struggle when a start-up business turned sour. "God has been faithful to continue to meet our needs, but it has been challenging," Scott said. "For the last eight years, we haven't made enough to be able to give much."

Yet, even in the most difficult financial times, Scott remained committed to giving. In a year of $27,000 in income, they dipped into savings and still gave away $25,000.

Scott and Kirsten have also been actively involved in peoples' lives through organizations like Campus Crusade for Christ. They have traveled overseas, including multiple return trips to Albania.

Scott shares his journey as often as someone will listen. "I always share my story. It's God's story," he said. Scott has seen Christ radically change lives around the globe. His stories are inspiring and often jaw-dropping. He led a man to Christ minutes before the man had planned to shoot his wife. He has influenced leading politicians in Albania. And he has seen generosity take root in his children.

"Whatever God tells you to do, no matter how big or impossible it seems, just go for it and then hang on and watch what He does. He wants to connect with you, to reveal Himself to you, and to work His power in you and through you. All we have to do is say yes, and put our fears aside," Scott said. "I've realized you're never going to experience the thrill of the Christian life—the abundant life that Christ promised to give us—unless you have the courage to line up your life with what the Word of God says, trust Him, and get so far out there that you're doomed to fail unless God does something miraculous."

Your Story:

1. Are you taking any risks in your giving that require a miracle? Commit to radical giving and ask God to help you trust Him in the process.

2. Do you have giving goals? Pray about how much you should give this year and make a plan. Write down three practical steps to get there:

   1. _____

   2. _____

   3. _____

3. At different points in Scott's story, God convicted him of his lifestyle, moved him out of contentment, and told him to wait. Listen to God's calling on your life right now. What is He telling you?

CHAPTER FIVE

Leaving It in the Offering Plate

Jim Fordyce

THE FIRST TIME Jim Fordyce gave a substantial amount of money to his church he thought he had made a huge mistake. He began to panic as the collection plate carried away his check.

"If I wouldn't have embarrassed myself, I probably would have dove down the aisle and took it back," Jim said.

Jim was miserable, convinced he had made a horrible financial decision. The next day he received a bank statement and discovered he had more money in his account than he thought. To his surprise, the difference was the exact amount of the check he had given at church. "It just hit me right then and there, I can't out-give God," Jim said.

As Jim is the chairman of the board for a Kansas City-based company and a partner in a holding company, he especially loves the strategic side of business. After owning his own companies, Jim decided to capitalize on consulting projects and partnering in businesses. He has been involved with as many as eight businesses at one time. "My focus has been primarily as a generalist, strategic and financial, getting businesses up and running," Jim said. "I have a very curious mind; I like to know how things work."

When Jim initially began to realize success in business, giving back to God was merely an afterthought. "Every Sunday I was faithfully putting my one dollar bill in the plate thinking I was giving a nod to God," he said. After God's faithfulness with that first large gift, Jim's perspective about generosity began to change. He realized that everything he had came from God.

Meat and Potatoes

As Jim became more sensitive to teachings about tithing and giving, he started taking more opportunities to be generous. "It was painful at first and a real act of faith," he said. Jim and one of his business partners grew a company for twelve years and eventually had the opportunity to sell.

Before the sale, Jim did something he'd never done before; he gave away part of the business to a giving fund. By doing so, Jim gained a significant tax advantage, but he also made God a literal and legal owner in the business. "For someone who owns a company and is about to do something with it, I think it's a fantastic choice," he said. "It saves you some taxes and helps get you some liquidity to do things for God's work."

Jim and his wife, Linda, use the majority of their resources to give to churches, Christian schools, and individual missionaries. "Most of our giving has been day-to-day operational," Jim explained. "It has just been our personality and nature to be meat-and-potatoes kind of people."

> "It has just been our personality and nature to be meat-and-potatoes kind of people."

Keeping things running is no menial task. When their church lacked the funds to finish a building project, Jim used his business expertise to devise a solution. He created a company with the investments of other church members and used the business to lend money to the church. "There was a lot of prayer in that one. It was a significant leap of faith, not just because of what I had at risk, but more importantly, being the fiduciary for others."

The plan allowed the church to finish the building project and repay its investors, including interest. "The thing worked perfectly, not because I was smart, but because God wanted it."

Although Jim has often experienced God's provision, he has struggled to tithe during times of unemployment. However, "I thank God that He gave me the courage to do it," Jim said. "Whatever came to me, we gave 10 percent back to the church. I never missed a meal, and never, ever in my life been late for a payment on anything."

The Business Ministry

Jim is passionate about business ministry largely because of his own testimony. Growing up, Jim's family attended church once a year. Linda accepted Christ after they were married, and Jim went to church primarily at her request. One morning at 5 AM, Jim was already sitting at his office desk. He decided to pray to accept Christ. "I didn't hear the Mormon Tabernacle Choir; I wasn't transfigured; so I figured, well, I'm just still not good enough to be a Christian. I'll try again tomorrow."

That same morning, a Christian businessman showed up at Jim's door and helped assure Jim of his salvation. "In retrospect, it is obvious that God had just led him there to help straighten out a guy who was confused," Jim said. "Here was a very successful businessman who was sensitive to how the Holy Spirit was leading him to influence the lives of other businessmen."

Jim now knows his skills and talents are gifts from God. He has learned to live generously with his most precious resource: time. He has been involved with Christian business ministries in Kansas City, taken leadership roles at his church, and given evenings and weekends to board meetings and roundtables. "God has blessed me with the talents I have, and if that involves me sacrificing some time in giving it back, so be it."

Not Slowing Down

Now in his late sixties, Jim continues to hold his life with an open hand. After twenty-five years in Kansas City, God led Jim and

Linda to move to rural Montana to help a small church and minister in the community. They decided to make a move that, in the world's eyes, simply didn't make sense. Yet, it's all a part of the adventure.

The change from metropolitan Kansas City to a town of four-hundred gives the Fordyces many chances to get involved in the community. "Our desire by being in the community and working side-by-side with people is that we will have the opportunity to share our faith and hopefully either lead them to Christ, help them in discipleship, or get them into our church, where they can hear the Word of God preached." He laughed and added, "We are not sitting around watching the fish swim."

Jim's life continues to be an adventure as he surrenders his money, time, and expertise and allows God to make him into a model of generosity. Leaving his check in the offering plate that Sunday morning may have been one of the best decisions he has made.

Your Story:

1. Time is one of our most valuable assets. Evaluate how you spend your time, and ask God what sacrifices you could **make to serve Him.**

2. Like the businessman who influenced Jim, are you listening to the Holy Spirit in your life? Who is God asking you to minister to right now?

3. Do you consider your occupation as ministry? Why or why not?

4. Jim and Linda are not slowing down with ministry in this next stage of life. How is God asking you to serve Him in this season of your life?

CHAPTER SIX

Reckless Young Love and Cancer

Megan Finnell

PEOPLE WERE WORRIED. Her family and friends trusted her, but they were concerned about her well-being. Megan was twenty-four and in love with a man who had cancer. "I loved him, and I wanted to be with him. I never wanted to be without him."

A Bond of Brokenness

Not long before Megan met Brandon, she told God she wanted to love people so much it made her weird. She could not have predicted where God would lead her willingness to love recklessly.

Megan met Brandon at a church band practice. He was the new drummer, he was cute, and he was single. She never would have guessed he was sick. After all, he wasn't the only bald guy in the room, she teased. Brandon openly shared his brokenness with Megan as he told her about his fight with cancer. "He was very gentle … very humble," Megan said.

She could relate to Brandon's pain. Megan, a vocal performance major, had developed vocal issues, which ended her professional singing career before it really began. "I told him about my own brokenness of having everything in my life, the whole trajectory, torn apart and having to learn who I was without a talent, who I was without all the pluses," Megan said.

Megan and Brandon connected on a deep level right away. It only took a couple dates for Megan to see how much she admired him. "His heart for people and for God and the authenticity of his life was just so attractive," she said.

Truly Living

Megan was well aware of what she risked (a future, pain, children) by dating a man with cancer. As she prayed about their developing relationship, the Lord placed John 12:25 on her heart: "In the same way, anyone who holds on to life just as it is destroys that life. But if you let it go, *reckless in your love*, you'll have it forever, real and eternal" (MSG, emphasis added).

"I think so many of us cling to life just as it is, but we need to let it go and be reckless in our love to have the full, forever-life that God wants us to have," Megan said. In a situation that screamed for self-protection, Megan chose to freely give her love to Brandon at any cost. "It was always scary, but I knew that no matter what—even if I lost, even if God didn't heal him—God would still carry me through. It was worth it."

Feeling God's peace to move forward, Megan and Brandon began dating. Their courtship was unusual, filled with uncertainty and frequent visits to the hospital. Nevertheless, Megan remained by Brandon's side. Through such unpredictable times, Megan learned to let go of her own life. "It was the most satisfied I have ever felt because I knew my whole life was in God's hands and in His control," she said. "I felt like I was living life more abundantly than I ever had before."

Brandon's attitude was the same. When a friend asked him if he was excited to get over cancer, so he could start living again, Brandon responded, "I have never lived more. This is what life is about; this is living life to the fullest."

> "This is what life is about; this is living life to the fullest."

Six months into dating, it seemed Brandon's condition was improving. His treatment was going well; his hair was growing back. Hopeful and in love, Brandon asked Megan to marry him. "In the days that he did have left, no matter if it was two weeks or twenty years, I wanted to have all of it," Megan said.

One month later, the couple received difficult news. "He went back for a scan and found that a very small amount of cancer had not been eradicated. It had started growing back."

Generosity and Grief

Brandon needed to go to Houston for more treatment. Not wanting to be separated, the couple decided to get married before he left and planned their wedding in two weeks. Megan saw true generosity from family, friends, and church members who made the wedding a reality. "Over two hundred people came from all over the world to the wedding. It was the most beautiful thing," she said. "All these people came to support and love him."

They didn't know it then, but it would be last time for many to see Brandon. Two days after the wedding, his condition worsened. Brandon never recovered enough to travel to Houston. Merely two-and-a-half months into married life, Brandon passed away.

Megan, only in her mid-twenties, was suddenly a grieving widow meeting with lawyers, making funeral arrangements, and growing up too fast. She faced agonizing pain and deep sadness, but she would have married Brandon again in a heartbeat. "My only regret is that we didn't have more time together."

Megan began to rebuild her life on her own. However, she was far from alone. Her Christian community surrounded her in a way she had never experienced before. Six months after Brandon's death Megan went to Colorado to spread his ashes, planning to move out of their apartment when she returned. In her absence, women from her church rented a moving truck and gathered more than thirty people to help.

"They packed up my apartment, unloaded it into my new house, cleaned my apartment, and locked it up so that when I came back, I could start over with a new life," she said. "People showed generosity such as I have never seen before or since. I think when you are the recipient of that much generosity, support, and help, you just want to be that to other people."

Rebuilding

Guilt, anger, and pain all surfaced as Megan continued to deal with the reality of Brandon's death. She moved through the grief as she faced many changes and uncertainties. Megan is relearning what it means to let go of her life as she finds that living and loving recklessly has become harder as she has gotten older.

"It's an ongoing struggle for me because I find myself holding so tightly to life as it is now that I don't give it away. I don't let it go, and I'm not reckless in my love because I think there is too much to lose. But in reality, there is *nothing* to lose; there is only ... gain."

The temptation to control her life may persist, and the grief may return—sometimes daily. However, Megan has tasted where true life in God is found. "Sacrifice is about giving up something you love for something you love more," she said. "We have to let go to find what we really want."

Your Story:

1. Megan has learned that loving recklessly is always worth it. Who in your life is God asking you to love well—without considering the cost?

2. Generosity is more than giving money. Take time to process Megan's story. How is God calling you into a holistic life of generosity?

3. Can you relate to the pain and loss Megan experienced? How are you allowing God and other people to carry you through?

4. Look around you and see who's hurting. Ask God to show you how to use your time, love, and compassion to serve those people.

CHAPTER SEVEN

Farmland Generosity

Austin & Rhoda Heise

AUSTIN AND RHODA Heise understand hard work. They made their living as Kansas farmers, tending the land God gave them through years when they had very little. Sitting side by side in their cozy retirement community home, the Heises' farming days are behind them. God blessed their faithfulness, and now they use their resources to spread the gospel. "We had all this land God had given to us," Rhoda said. "We had been blessed in many ways, not only financially, but with good health. So it really needed to go back to Him."

Austin and Rhoda grew up in difficult times with little surplus, but their families still made it a priority to give back to God. "My parents always gave. They always talked about the tenth. Giving was an important thing," Rhoda said. "We learned from other people who would bring us groceries or meat how important giving was to the person who received it."

Austin came to Christ during a revival meeting at his childhood church in Kansas, and Rhoda accepted her Savior during a tent meeting in Ontario, Canada. The two met at college in California and have been married more than sixty years. After graduating, they moved to a farm in northeast Kansas.

Austin farmed the land; Rhoda raised their three children and taught second graders for more than twenty years. Even when money was tight, the Heises were as dedicated to giving as they were to their farm. "In the early years, it was very tough on the farm," Rhoda said. "We came in the 50s, out of college, and we had four or five straight years of drought. We had basically nothing. Then there were some good years. It took us about forty years to really feel we got on top."

Life's Work

After years of hard, faithful work, the Heises began to see the fruit of their labor. The farm did well, and they acquired more land. When they decided to move from the farm into town, the Heises desired to do something different with their property than most farmers. "As we heard people talk, their idea was just to give the farm to their children," Austin explained. "I think, in many cases, the family doesn't need it."

Though the Heises plan to leave some land to their family, they view God's Kingdom as their first priority. "All our life, we intended to give back what had been given to us," Austin said. Rhoda added, "You begin to know your years are less, and you aren't taking any of it with you."

> "You begin to know your years are less, and you aren't taking any of it with you."

The Heises started looking for ways to use their land for God. They began pursuing a plan to give away some of the farm. Their plan was, of course, contrary to the familiar saying, "Don't give away the farm." Even with their stewardship mindset, giving up their farm was difficult. It represented the work of their lives—their struggle and their success. Austin walked that land for many years, watching the crops grow.

"He always likes to do the math; he likes the marketing because he has always been a businessman," Rhoda said. So Austin began working with an attorney with expertise in charitable giving, but who also had sensitivity to their feelings and the fact that the farm represented their life work. The plan was to give away part of the farm. By giving away part of the farm, they could still allow farming to continue on the portion they kept. Also, the gift produced a significant tax benefit for them. It made sense.

Ultimately, they donated a portion of the land to a giving fund. A buyer was found, the property sold, and the proceeds went into their fund. Through their fund, they now can give to multiple ministries.

> "The plan was to give away part of the farm."

Giving Back

With new resources to give, the Heises found new joy in giving. "We hear about people who are hungry or suffering, and we like to help them. In addition we like to see the message of the gospel go out to other parts of the world," Austin said. Their giving fund has allowed them to partner in new buildings and special programs for the ministries they value.

"It would have been easy to give this farm to one organization," Austin said. "I am sure it would have been effective, and we would still have the same tax benefits, but by placing it in a giving fund, we can give to various projects as they come along."

Rhoda added, "These tax benefits not only benefit us, but they also benefit the Kingdom. There is more money in the Kingdom because we were able to reduce our tax burden while giving more."

The Heises attend ministry functions and host individuals they sponsor. They enjoy hearing about how their gifts have been used. "Not that we need to be recognized for what we have given, but it blesses us to know how it blessed [the ministries we support]," Rhoda said. "It encourages us to go on and do some more."

The Heises desire to pass on their heart for generosity to their children and grandchildren. One Christmas, the Heises gave each of their seven grandchildren $100 to give to any cause they wished. They asked their grandchildren to report back to them where they gave the money and how it made them feel. "We wanted them to experience the joy of giving," Rhoda said. "I hope it helped them to enjoy the giving process and to get them started."

The Heises see giving back to God as a blessing. In this season of their lives, they can watch their hard work fund God's work in the future. "It is wonderful to be able to have something to give," Rhoda said. "We ourselves can't go out and work in a lot of the places where this money will go. We spent our lives making this. This is what God called us to do. Now it belongs to Him."

Your Story:

1. What is your life's work? How is God asking you to use it for His Kingdom?

2. How are you passing on a heart for generosity to the next generation?

3. What assets could God be calling you to place at His feet? Pray and seek wise counsel about ways you can use your resources for God during your lifetime.

CHAPTER EIGHT

The Greatest Asset

Steve Trice

IN FIVE YEARS, Steve Trice lost nine people to cancer, including his mother and father. Steve worked hard to stay healthy, but then he was also diagnosed with cancer. "I was a work-out-aholic. I ate the right foods. I did all the right things and still I found that I had cancer at age thirty-nine," Steve said. "I thought that was my death sentence. I didn't think it was fair."

Even with a great marriage, two kids, and a successful business, Steve suffered from depression throughout his thirties. By the time he faced cancer, he saw little reason to hope. Even after he had surgery, he was convinced the cancer would win in the end. "It always came back, and it always got the others, so I believed that would happen to me too." Steve's stability was shaken. He began to reevaluate his life, wondering what value it really had.

"My career, my wife, and my children were my life. There was an emptiness in me; there was depression, anxiety, and constant worry," he said. "I felt like my ladder was up against the wrong wall."

One morning, Steve attended a prayer breakfast for businessmen. After hearing a speaker share about how Christ had changed his life, Steve discovered what he had been searching for. He accepted Christ at age forty-three.

"I have seen my worldview change, and everything that I do has changed. Jesus Christ has taken control of my life," he said. "I now know clearly what my purpose is. I know where I'm going, and I know why I'm going there."

An Impossible Deal

Steve's total surrender to Christ is evident in his language. He refers to his business as the company he stewards. "It's all about Him, and He is doing great things with it. I just show up," Steve said.

Steve started Jasco Products Company, LLC, in 1975. In 1998, the business started using the GE brand under a license from the General Electric Company, which Steve called a miracle in itself. Five years later, GE offered to sell its home electrical products company to Jasco. The GE business was twice the size of Steve's Oklahoma business, and GE wanted it operational in just ninety days. Incredulous, Steve said he would pray about it. GE told him to hurry.

"It was an impossible task," Steve said. "Many banks weren't even going to talk to us about it because it was too fast." Steve fell to his knees in prayer. The deal excited him, but he knew it would ultimately fail unless it was God's will.

"I didn't know how we would find facilities to house it. I didn't know how we would ever hire enough people. I didn't know how we would be able to serve all the customers it would entail," he said. "It was a huge, huge risk to buy a business twice as large as the company we were running in a completely different industry—a business we didn't know or understand."

Steve decided to present the opportunity to thirteen people he trusted—including his wife, executive staff, accountants, attorneys, and his spiritual advisor. He decided he would ask them to give him their opinions through secret ballot. If he received at least twelve affirmatives, he would go through with the deal. Steve was fifty-seven years old, and he and his wife, NeAnn, had begun talking about early retirement around that time. He was convinced she would oppose the idea. To his surprise, her response was, "We have to do it."

When Steve received affirmation from the other twelve, he had no doubt that this was what God wanted. He and his team began to tackle the challenge. They needed to borrow six times more money than they ever had before. They needed 400,000 square feet to move five GE warehouses to Oklahoma City, and only two facilities in the city could offer adequate space. They had to hire 105 people, finance the property and the acquisition, and prepare their systems to deliver to major mass merchandisers they had never worked with before.

"We had literally seventy-six business days to get it done. It was impossible."

But with God, all things are possible. "Ten thousand things fell into place. It was God's will. Period," Steve said. "Through that process, He has taught me that this business belongs to Him, that He can do great things with it."

Relinquishing Control

Before Steve learned to steward his business, he viewed giving as simply a part of his civic duty. After coming to Christ, Steve was discipled by businessmen who taught him what God's Word says about tithing and giving. Steve began tithing on his salary, his bonuses, and eventually on the corporate profits as well.

"I'll never forget when we started tithing off of corporate profits," he said. "I had a death grip on that check at 11:59 PM on New Year's Eve. I let it go, and twelve days later—through some circumstances that virtually had nothing to do with our business—we received back seven-and-a-half times that check. God let me know on that day: *You can't out-give Me*."

> "I'll never forget when we started tithing off of the corporate profits."

Steve learned to pry his fingers off his business. He and NeAnn were challenged to take their giving to a new level after attending a Generous Giving conference. As a result of hearing several testimonies at that conference, Steve and NeAnn began thinking about giving away some of the assets of the business—not just cash. This was a new thing to them.

Eventually, they met with the National Christian Foundation, where they learned how they could give a portion of their assets (whether stock in the business or real estate), receive tax benefits, and increase their giving at the same time. However, Steve dealt with reservations and skepticism when he first considered giving assets he had owned for more than thirty years.

Busyness also threatened his desire to move forward in generosity. "There's that constant nagging that you will get it done someday, but I'm too busy today," he recalled. However, as Steve stayed in the Word, God solidified these decisions through the promises in Proverbs 3:9–10 and 2 Corinthians 9:6–14 that discuss honoring the Lord with one's wealth and giving cheerfully.

"It's not about a prosperity gospel," Steve said. "If you will step out in faith, He will meet your every need, and you will have more to give. One great freeing principle my sons and I have learned is how to determine 'How much is enough?' We decided how much we needed to support our lifestyles and eventual retirement. So instead of always striving to acquire more, we simply give the rest away. Wow, what a great relief, freedom, and feeling that is!"

With the support of his wife, Christian attorneys, accountants, and his two sons who are involved in the business, Steve followed through and gave away a portion of their assets.

> "God has given Christian businessmen a place."

"God has given Christian businessmen a place," he said. "That's why He's got those businesses, and He can't wait to bless them. He has blessed ours incredibly. It has grown ten times in the last eleven years, and it is doing very well."

The Greatest Assets

Besides the visible blessings on his business, Steve has seen God use his company to change the lives of individuals. An employee named Anthony stopped Steve one day and asked to speak with him. Anthony told Steve he grew up in church, but it wasn't until working at Jasco Products that he learned how to have a personal relationship with Christ. The company paid for Anthony and his wife to attend a marriage conference, where his wife also accepted Christ. The best part, Anthony said, was that his eight-year-old daughter had started reading the Bible.

"I had to come to Jasco Products Company to learn about a personal and intimate relationship with Jesus Christ," Anthony said. "That's the effect that Jasco Products had on me and my family."

Stories like Anthony's, and Steve's own testimony, have led Steve to focus his giving on marketplace ministry. "The Lord has ministered to us in specific ways, so He wants us to turn around and give in the specific ways we have been ministered to," Steve said. "Before I came to know Christ, I—as probably most all businessmen—would tell you that our greatest asset was our people. Those were words, but I was really leveraging people to make money for me and my family."

Today, people really are Jasco's greatest asset. Steve dedicates company time and money to spreading the gospel of Christ and discipling men and women in the marketplace. "We have people their best hours of the day," Steve said. To make the most of that time, the company facilitates education in line with people's career goals by giving them full scholarships to a local Christian university. Jasco also provides biblically based training regarding marriage, raising children, and managing money.

"We teach our people how to give of their time, their talent, and their treasure and help them develop their relationships with their spouse, their children, and their Lord."

Steve has also developed ways to encourage employees to live generously. "If they will give thirty hours a year to their choice of local ministries, we'll match that with $300. If they will give up to $500 to local ministries other than their church, we will match that $500."

After forty-three years of living and working for his own benefit, Steve's life was changed by Christ and by the businessmen who were willing to invest in him. His view of the workplace has also changed drastically. His company belongs to God, and people are much more than a means to an end for Steve.

"It's not about the transactions; the transactions only facilitate the ministry. The fruit is the eternal impact we have on another person's life while we're here on earth. It's about Anthony, his wife, his children, and his future generations. That's the business that we're in."

Your Story:

1. Are people really your business's greatest asset? How are you encouraging your employees or co-workers to give of their time, talents, and treasure?

2. Have you relinquished control of your business or job? How can people tell that your business and career truly belong to God?

3. Steve is learning that it's all about the individual. Pay attention to your employees and co-workers this week. Ask God to show you their needs. Look for opportunities to bless people. Write down three people from work and commit to praying for them this week:

   - _____

   - _____

   - _____

CHAPTER NINE

A GM Dealer's Road to Generosity

Randy Reed

WHEN GENERAL MOTORS faced uncertain times, Randy Reed knew he could lose both of his GM dealerships. However, God paved the way for him through GM's dark days. "We didn't end up losing either one. We had some of the best years we have ever had during that time," Randy said. Giving back to the Lord is a priority in Randy's life, and he said there is no denying the Lord's hand in his business.

"When the opportunity came up to buy another dealership in the midst of a recession, we were sitting in a financial position where we could take advantage of that," he said. "I think God is helping us. I see that very directly, and I think my key people see it too. They see the difference it has made."

Protection and Blessing

After working for his dad's car dealership in Iowa, Randy moved to Kansas City with enough money to make a down payment on a GM store. He and his wife, Karen, began the faith journey of running a business and raising a family. Early on, Randy and Karen realized the auto industry was an opportunity for ministry. "We didn't understand that really well, but we felt that God was going to use us and our lives through our business," Randy said.

> "We felt the Lord was going to use us and our lives through our business."

Randy learned about giving growing up, but he didn't take the concept of tithing to heart until his late twenties. "When we made the decision to tithe, I began to tithe out of the net of our check—the after-taxes part," he said. "After hearing further teaching, we learned that it was the firstfruits, so we took that last extra step to make it right. That has been a point of no return after my wife and I decided to do that." As they stepped forward with tithing, the Reeds began to see God's blessings in their lives. "We sensed there was a connection between the giving we did to the Lord and the blessings we had in our lives—not just financial things," Randy said.

One profound moment came when he and his wife returned to Iowa for a visit. A neighbor told them the basement in their old house had flooded—something that never happened while they lived there. "We were thinking, 'Wow, this never happened to us,' and the Lord spoke to me and said, 'Because you tithe,'" Randy recalled. "I have no idea what God has protected us from over the years." Although they do not give to get, Randy believes there is real reward in a life of giving.

"I believe that generosity ushers God's blessing back into your life," he said. "Many times, the blessing is a good marriage, children, friends—the things that are really important in life. Maybe it is some money also, but that's really not the purpose for giving to God."

Tithing was simply a discipline at first for Randy, but God has continued to engage his heart, bringing him into a new kind of generosity. "Even one dollar more than [what I gave previously], God is saying, 'Yes, that's great, Randy!' God rejoices with any generosity—big and small doses."

Beyond the Tithe

As tithing became ingrained in their hearts, Randy and Karen began to take step after step in obedience. God led them from tithing, to giving beyond the tithe, to making faith promises—pledging money they didn't have at the time. As his first faith promise, Randy pledged to give an amount as part of a church capital campaign. He and Karen agreed on the pledge which they both acknowledged was beyond anything they could reasonably fulfill without God's intervention.

God did in fact intervene. Randy had another company approach him about buying him out of a lease he held on another property. Randy prayed and felt like God was leading him to ask for a price that Randy himself considered too high. Randy presented the price to the other company, and surprisingly, they accepted. When the deal closed, the company explained a series of "coincidences" that had allowed them to pay the price they admitted was too high. The money allowed Randy to fulfill his pledge. "That was a real faith-builder for us, seeing how God answered those leadings of His. He provided the funds to be able to give through business opportunities and other ways."

Learning to Give

Randy and Karen work together to determine where the Lord is calling them to give. "We want to give to high-impact ministries," Randy said. "There are so many ministries out there that use money really well."

Randy said they have scattered many seeds instead of focusing on a single ministry. Randy has taken both of his sons on mission trips to China and Russia, and he has traveled to Haiti with the Global Orphan Project. His family also built and funded an orphanage in Uganda. Although it takes great prayer and discernment, Randy and Karen have also learned when to say no to giving.

"I think we have learned that if you give a ministry money, and you aren't led to do it, it is not really going to be a blessing for you or them," Randy said. "But if they end up connecting with the right donor who helps them in a significant way, there is that heart connection. That's the full deal we like to see happen."

The Reeds choose to do much of their giving anonymously. "It is freeing in a way," Randy said. "God sees it, you feel good about it, and you don't have to worry about them saying thank you or anything like that."

For Randy, generosity has shifted from obedience to a lifestyle. "Generosity is a way of life and the way a person is—the opposite of holding onto things, but giving freely," Randy said. "Generosity is letting God flow through you."

Randy seeks to instill this attitude in his employees at his dealership. "What I try to encourage is that being generous may just be helping one of your teammates when he is busy with a customer," Randy said.

As Randy has followed God down the road of generosity, he has experienced blessings and protection, and he wants to continue to answer God's call. "The answer is always yes. I hope I can walk that out the rest of my life."

Your Story:

1. Where have you seen God's protection and blessing in your life? Do you see a correlation between that and your generosity?

2. How do you view tithing? Is it an obligation or joy? Do you give out of your firstfruits? Consider what shift you may need to make in your giving to take that next step in obedience.

3. Do you choose to give in name or anonymously? Do you tend to scatter your giving or focus on one area? Spend time in prayer and talk to your family about how you handle your giving.

CHAPTER TEN

God's Money After an Airline Tragedy

James & Kristen

KRISTEN* WAS A singer. At twenty-two, vocal performance was a much deeper part of her than merely her undergraduate degree. "It was wrapped up in the fabric of who I felt I was and who God had created me to be," Kristen said.

She was planning to use music for the rest of her life. She and her boyfriend, James, had just started planning their lives together, dreaming about how God could use their shared love of music. Together, they would go to graduate school, then on to perform.

But one day changed everything.

Only one month after her senior voice recital, Kristen was returning from an overseas trip with her choir ensemble. As James waited in the airport to welcome her home, he heard the plane had been delayed. Half an hour. An hour. Time passed and still no sight of the plane. Gradually, news trickled in—there had been an accident. James imagined the worst.

Kristen's plane had crashed in a thunderstorm. Eleven of the 130 passengers died, including two of Kristen's friends.

Last name omitted by request.

Kristen escaped from the horror of the burning wreckage with her life, but she would never perform again. Kristen was on a ventilator for a week, and she suffered extensive lung damage and scars on her vocal cords. Severe burns on her hands and right arm required skin grafts. Daily life became a struggle as Kristen's time was dedicated to healing both physically and emotionally. Life suddenly became very serious and intense for James and Kristen's young dating relationship.

> "Kristen escaped from the horror of the burning wreckage with her life, but she would never perform again."

"The stakes were a lot higher because I was dealing with a lifelong injury," Kristen said. The reality of her injuries drastically changed their vision for a future together. "We were musicians, so that had been something we were both very passionate about—something we didn't just have in common, but we thought could be our common calling. God could use us in so many ways together," Kristen said. "Losing my music was just crushing in many, many ways."

James was going to California for the summer, but he sat by Kristen's hospital bed before he left. Though she couldn't answer him, James said, "Kristen, I love you, and I'm committed to you. I will see you soon."

A Void

At first, Kristen lived in euphoria, thankful to be alive and amazed by God's goodness. But by the end of her two-month hospitalization, she began to slip into a dark depression. "I just retreated within and tried to disconnect myself from my emotions because everything was just so sorrowful and so intense," she said. Instead of returning to school in the fall, Kristen stayed home and concentrated on recovering. Her days were filled with counseling appointments and hand and voice therapy.

"It was just one thing after another of continuing sorrow upon sorrow—different friends that we lost due to injuries, and the beginning of bitterness and anger toward the airlines for poor decisions and what was an obvious error that led to the crash," Kristen said.

Though she longed to believe God was still good, Kristen wrestled with feeling His presence. She fought to feel anything besides depression, anger, and despair. "At times, I would cry out to God in desperation because I had nothing within me to feel connected to Him," Kristen said. "Anything that would make me feel hope, encouragement, or peace was far out of my grasp. I would read God's Word, and it would fall flat. I felt so abandoned by God. I felt so rejected. I felt so picked on. I felt so punished."

Unprecedented Wealth

When Kristen returned to school, she had to adjust to a new normal. Due to her skin grafts, Kristen had to wear tight-fitting pressure garments twenty-three hours a day, making even simple tasks extremely difficult.

Yet, James and Kristen remained committed to each other. The couple got engaged and quickly found themselves facing more life-altering decisions. As a couple, James and Kristen decided to sue the airlines. "A lot of people get engaged, and they pick out china," Kristen said. "Before we were even engaged, we were trying to decide whether to get involved in major litigation."

The council of lawyers representing the survivors told Kristen they would take her case first. Wanting to get married before the trial, Kristen and James planned a wedding in two-and-a-half months. They were married on May 6, 2000, about eleven months after the crash.

Then, only three months after their wedding, Kristen sat before a jury and recounted with horrific detail the damage done to her body and her dreams. "I think the airline didn't know what to do with me because, at that point, I was so broken and starting to be so angry that the money didn't matter," Kristen said. "No amount of money could make what happened okay."

But money was all that the airline had to give. Kristen received the largest award for personal damages ever given in her state at the time. The young couple found themselves wealthier than they had ever dreamed, far from the lives they had imagined as middle class professors and musicians.

"I almost hated the money at first because it was this big check, and then they were done with me," Kristen said. "They could move on, and I was still stuck in the aftermath with my body shattered, my dreams shattered, my life forever changed, and still feeling so alienated from my faith and from God."

> "I almost hated the money at first because it was this big check, and then they were done with me."

The Search for Normalcy

After everything they had been through, James and Kristen struggled to find where they, millionaires in their early twenties, fit into the world. They used the money to pay Kristen's medical bills, but pushed aside the weight of their wealth for some time. "We didn't know what it meant to not have to work for money or to not have struggles similar to my other colleagues in grad school, for example," James said.

"The first few years we were very cautious, didn't want to do anything drastic, didn't want to make any decisions we would regret, didn't know how to handle that kind of money," James said. "We were pretty secretive about it; we hardly told anybody."

James and Kristen focused instead on their marriage, James' work in graduate school, and Kristen's continued recovery. "I was still struggling with my own personal battles of bitterness, so I was paranoid and upset about everything and really sensitive to people's comments like, 'So James is in grad school. What do you do?'" Kristen recalled.

Although they could have bought any house or any car they desired, Kristen thanks God for protecting them from those temptations. "By God's grace, He made it very clear that there was not going to be any healing or happiness found in the material wealth; that only healing and true joy could come from Him," she said.

From Resentment to Humility

James and Kristen were generous with their money from the beginning, but over the years, God began to show them exciting possibilities for using their wealth. "Even though I hated the money at first, now I was seeing it as this unbelievable opportunity to do unbelievable things for God's Kingdom. I felt so humbled by that," Kristen said. "Who am I that we can write this check, or build this building, or partner in this way? Who are we that we can do these things? He is doing these things; we just have such a small part to play, and we are so humbled by it."

James and Kristen learned to be patient as God invited them into the process of deciding how and where to give. Eventually God led them to a passion for widows and orphans. James has also developed a love for business as missions.

"At first it was frustrating because we didn't know ... we had to figure it out. We felt like God should tell us what to do with the money and then we would do it," James said. "I'm the kind of guy who really looks for value. I want to know the money is making a difference, and I'm using it well and wisely. God cares about that. He has allowed me to be that way and be the kind of involved person who would get to know where the money goes."

God used a trip to Thailand to continue to heal Kristen's bitter, hurt heart. Ten years after the crash, Kristen listened to the stories of women rescued out of sex trafficking. She related to their pain and saw God's restoration in their lives. "That was a real turning point for me," she said. "If this person survived this unbelievable injustice done on purpose by somebody evil; if they can receive God's mercy and live a life of forgiveness and freedom, how dare I not?"

The trip transformed Kristen's resentment about the money into humility. "It pushed me over the edge of being okay with it to actually being grateful for it because these girls will never be able to stand in front of a courtroom and hold somebody accountable for the injustices done to them."

A Valuable Inheritance

Kristen and James have already seen generous spirits sprouting up in their three young children, and they are excited to continue to teach them about giving. "We are not guaranteed tomorrow. I learned that at twenty-two," Kristen said. "I think the most passionate ministry James and I have right now is our children and teaching them about generosity. Not because they know we have a lot, but because they know what we have is God's and we are accountable to Him."

One tangible way Kristen and James teach their children generosity is by sponsoring World Vision children who share the same birthdays as each of their kids. When their kids ask for something they want, Kristen and James gently challenge them by asking, "Is that a good use of God's money?" Their kids often point to the pictures on the fridge and say, "*That's* a good use of God's money!"

After nearly ten years of learning to grow into their new skin, Kristen and James are looking forward to pursuing generosity even more. They have attended Generous Giving conferences where they realized their potential for igniting generosity in others. "That has encouraged us to not be as secretive about what we do because it does spur one another on," Kristen said. "I'm excited to embrace who we are. This is a part of our story."

They are humbled by the opportunities they have to partner in God's work, feeling like they are merely on the brink of how He wants to use them. The physical pain is now a distant memory for Kristen. She may never have all her questions answered, but she has tasted God's goodness and chooses to trust Him each day.

"On a personal level, it has been an unbelievable journey of faith. As a family and as a couple, we are so completely unified because of this ride of learning to be generous," Kristen said. "It has been incredibly unifying because we have seen how God can bring such good out of such tragedy. I didn't think He could redeem this. But He has, and He is so good! We are so excited about what we can do in our lifetime to build God's Kingdom. I wouldn't trade that for anything."

Your Story:

1. Take time to reflect on Kristen and James' story. They have experienced God's faithfulness in bringing blessings out of extreme sorrow. What pain have you faced in your life? Do you believe God can redeem your tragedies?

2. Are you holding on to hurt or bitterness? God wants to free you, and He's asking you to let it go. How can you take steps toward trusting Him with your heart?

3. No matter what is in your past, how is God asking you to embrace your story? How can you use your story to encourage others?

CHAPTER ELEVEN

Investors for God's Kingdom

Larry & Mandy Powell

L ARRY POWELL GREW up in a middle class Christian family in Texas, but it wasn't until his late forties that Christ became the Lord of his life. Even then, it took this investor time to relinquish control of his business.

Larry had a God-given passion to start his own company. When the opportunity arose, he followed his dream and opened an investment and portfolio management company. Although he was a Christian, Larry didn't always include God in his work. "At the time, I never thought that the business belonged to God," Larry said. "It was *mine*. I started it. I was the king of my little kingdom."

He managed investments for thirty-five years, holding on to the keys of his kingdom. It wasn't until after he met his wife, Mandy, that his mindset began to shift. Shortly before Mandy became pregnant with twin girls, the Powells took a stewardship class through Crown Financial Ministries, and God gave them a new perspective on following Him.

"Through this class, and being around like-minded people, we realized that everything we had—time, talent, resources—was all His," Larry said. "Because of this foundation where God was the owner, we started making changes in every part of our lives. God dropped the veil and showed us another way to live."

Larry and Mandy began to see generosity and finances in a whole new light—a change that eventually permeated Larry's business. "I realized I had carved out this little kingdom separate from God," he explained. "I was giving Him everything but my business. Once that light switch turned on, obviously the business was His also."

> "I realized I had carved out this little kingdom separate from God."

Larry began managing his company differently as he kept the desire to give back to God in the foreground. He put 20 percent of his company's stock in a giving fund. And over time, Larry discovered he was more passionate about God's Kingdom than his own.

However, Larry's business partners weren't experiencing the same transformation. As God continued to work on Larry's heart, he decided it was time to give up his company and start working for the Lord. Larry sold his business and retired. "That was such an easy decision because I didn't feel like it was fair to them, and I sensed that God was calling me."

Larry said these last few years have been the best of his life. "I had invested other peoples' money for so long—now it was time to manage what God had given us for Him and for the Kingdom. Instead of being a portfolio manager for other people, I was now a portfolio manager for God."

A New Business Development

When Larry and Mandy were first married, they described their giving as unplanned and scattered. With their new perspective on stewardship, they decided to meet with a financial advisor and develop a family mission statement. "We narrowed our giving passions and places we wanted to see influenced to three areas," Mandy said. "Those areas were the poor and needy, the sanctity of life, and the installation of a biblical worldview in young people."

The Powells have also dedicated their time to those same areas. Mandy has volunteered with a crisis pregnancy center, and Larry has worked with the Salvation Army. "Since I am an old investment guy, I like to say, 'Invest. Invest your time, talents, and resources for God's Kingdom,'" Larry said.

Larry and Mandy know they are still learning and growing, but they have enjoyed experimenting with new types of giving. Mandy started a giving circle with women in Kansas City. Each woman sacrificed something for a year and saved that money to give away.

"For a year I did not shop for myself other than just the necessities," she said. The women got together every other month and invited representatives from different charities to speak at their meetings. At the end of the year, they pooled their money and gave to some of those organizations. "It was neat because we learned about so many other charities out there. Also, because we were sacrificing something, it made giving more at the forefront of our minds," Mandy said.

Random Acts of Generosity

Another way Larry and Mandy practice generosity has become one of their favorites. They keep a small amount of cash on hand and seek out "random" opportunities to give. "We just pray for God to bring us someone who really needs it, and we keep our eyes open for people in need," Mandy explained. With this sensitivity to their surroundings, God leads them into conversations—often with strangers—where needs become obvious.

"The most fun is randomly giving," Larry said. "To see the look on someone's face who is not expecting it, to give it away, and let them know that this is not from me; it's from God. You're not only giving what you have, but you see the joy on their faces and get to share with them it's from God."

This spontaneous generosity has allowed the Powells to minister to others in unexpected ways. One of Larry's favorite experiences was giving money to five girls who were selling lemonade to raise money for tornado victims in Joplin, Missouri. "I handed the girl $100, and she said, 'I can't take this.' I said, 'Yes, you can, this is from God,'" Larry recalled. The girls were overjoyed. "That was the best $100 I ever spent."

The Generosity of Family

The Powells are also teaching their own girls that everything belongs to God. "You've got to expose them to it, because most people aren't born generous," Larry said. "Generosity is part of that biblical worldview that you have to instill in your kids."

> "Generosity is part of that biblical worldview that you have to instill in your kids."

The twins have picked up on generosity from watching Larry and Mandy give to strangers. One of their daughters wanted to empty her piggy bank and give everything she had to a special cause at their school. When Larry asked if she wanted to save any, she said no, she wanted to give it all. "It puts me to shame," Larry said. "We haven't given everything yet. She is ministering to us."

As Larry and Mandy raised their daughters, they realized that family and building family were key values for them. Since family has been such a blessing in their lives, they felt led to share that blessing with others. So, they decided to adopt three sisters (ages one, three, and five) from the Democratic Republic of the Congo. These three girls will soon join the twins and form a family of seven. The Powells' hope is that these girls will return to their homeland as missionaries someday.

Generosity in Larry's life has brought him closer to the Lord and given him a new perspective on everything he has been given. Larry and Mandy now find great joy in spending their time and resources to invest in God's Kingdom instead of their own. They have learned the true purpose for their wealth.

Larry said, "It's not a blessing unless you use it to glorify God. If you use it selfishly, it's a curse. It will take you down; it will take your family down; it will destroy your life if you use it just for yourself. But if you use it for God's glory, then it is a blessing."

Your Story:

1. Are you investing more in God's Kingdom than your own? What do you need to do to let go of the keys and give God control in your life?

2. Has wealth been a blessing or a curse in your family? How can you use your finances and your resources to bless others?

3. Challenge yourself to random generosity this week. Decide how much you are going to give and keep the cash on hand. Pray for God to lead you into a situation with a need and listen for His direction.

    Take time to journal about your experience. How did giving make you feel? What did you learn from the person you gave to? What did God teach you through this experience?

CHAPTER TWELVE

A Father of Faith

Thurman Mitchell Sr.

N O ONE CAN accuse Thurman Mitchell of having an easy life. He has struggled through times of little and lived through great tragedy, yet his life shines as a model of generosity. Born in 1924 on a farm north of Guthrie, Oklahoma, Thurman Mitchell Sr. was the sixth of nine children. In 1929, Thurman's father left for work and never returned home.

"He walked off—if it was on purpose or some kind of tragedy, no one ever knew," Thurman said. Thurman's oldest brother raised him and his siblings while their mother worked, struggling to provide for her children on $1 per day. Life was difficult on the farm, but the Mitchell children intently watched the service and example of their strong mother.

"I watched my mother leave when it was dark and come back when it was dark," Thurman said. "If I am the person that everyone says I am, first I have to give God the glory and praise, and then I also give my mother praise because she is my role model."

The Most Valuable Treasure

Thurman graduated from high school in 1942 and married his bride, Hazel, whom he had known throughout childhood. Thurman had been baptized in a river at age thirteen, but he didn't fully understand what it meant to have a relationship with Christ until Hazel challenged him.

"She said, 'The water did nothing for you whatsoever. You have to receive Christ into your life. It's Christ's death, burial, and resurrection—you have to believe that in order to be saved,'" he recalled. "I've never looked back since she really told me about how good Christ is, what He has done, what He is still doing, and what He will do. He is true to His Word. His grace and His mercy never, never fail."

Christ has brought Thurman incredible joy, and he has been living to serve Him for more than sixty years: "I've just got to serve Him the best I know how for the rest of my life."

A Character of Faithfulness

Shortly after Thurman and Hazel were married, Thurman joined the army as WWII raged in Europe. Leaving New York for England, Thurman watched the Statue of Liberty fade in the distance and prayed that God would bring him back to see that sight again.

Hazel gave birth to their firstborn, Thurman Mitchell Jr., while her husband was overseas. Thurman did return safely after three years of service. He attended Langston University in Langston, Oklahoma, on the GI Bill and obtained his degree in industrial arts. "That department simply taught brick laying, carpentering, electrical engineering, auto mechanics, just things you could do with your hands to make a living," Thurman said.

After graduating in 1952, Thurman did contract work with one of his brothers, but a segregated and prejudiced society pressed against him as an African-American. "I couldn't be admitted in the union because they said you had to have a voucher," he recalled. "There weren't any blacks in the union to vouch for you."

Thurman and Hazel had six children, Thurman Jr., Emmitt, Marjorie, Arnold, Dwayne, and Denzel. To provide for his family, Thurman took a labor-intensive construction job spreading concrete. Thurman began tithing in 1955 while making $1.25 an hour, and he has never missed a beat. He faithfully tithes on every hard-earned penny that comes into his hand.

"My concept of giving and supporting God's ministry is just from my heart. He has done so much for us; I've just got to support the ministry," he said. Of course, Thurman's concept of giving grew to extend well beyond cash. He gave himself.

The Peacemaker

When a position opened up in a Wichita, Kansas, school district, Thurman decided to apply. "Here again, because of the color of my skin, I couldn't get into that department at all," he said. Despite initial rejection, Thurman was eventually offered a job repairing school equipment.

"God is always in the plan. I always tried, to the best of my ability, to conduct myself as a gentleman and to be nice to people—to give and be a blessing." God honored his faithfulness. Thurman's love for people quickly gained him respect and even caught the attention of the head of the transportation department. Thurman was offered a position, and he eventually became the supervisor of transportation for the district.

> "I always tried, to the best of my ability, to conduct myself as a gentleman and to be nice to people."

"I was like a peacemaker," Thurman said. "If children had problems on buses, I would get with their parents, the school's administration, the students, and the bus driver and try to resolve the problem the best we could to keep those children in school."

Thurman served the district for sixteen years and retired in 1989. However, Thurman's love for helping people made him restless at home all day. When the district asked him to come back, he gladly accepted, leaving retirement after only a year. Thurman returned to work as a liaison for the bus company, where he continued to keep the peace and fight for children's education.

Father to the Community

Thurman loves Christ and has a passion for people. He has made the development of young people a priority in his life through his involvement with the school district, Boy Scouts, and his church. "Folks all over the city of Wichita, especially in my home church, all the young people, middle-aged folk, and some of the old folk call my wife and me 'Dad and Mom Mitchell,'" Thurman said. "I have so many spiritual daughters and sons it's amazing."

> "Folks all over the city ... call my wife and me 'Dad and Mom Mitchell.'"

During the desegregation of Wichita schools, Thurman continued to act as a peacemaker in his district and as a leader in his community. He was involved in the Civil Rights Movement and became one of the presidents of the National Association for the Advancement of Colored People in the city. He founded the Black Historical Society, led community development programs, and served as a treasurer and deacon in his church.

"I'm just serving God and getting joy out of doing it because God has been so good to me," he said. The city has recognized Thurman for his service on multiple occasions, and his son, Emmitt, said the turnout of his protégés and admirers is always overwhelming.

"In this area, he is very well known and highly thought of," Emmitt said. "He has many spiritual children that God has given him over the years that are, in many cases, closer to him than his own biological children. It always amazes us when we see those people around."

For years, Thurman and Hazel modeled generosity and hospitality by opening up their home. Thurman's pastor would consistently tell the congregation to head to the Mitchells' for a good Sunday dinner. "We didn't have very much growing up, but when God started blessing me, I've had as many as twenty-five or thirty people after church on Sundays come to our home to eat dinner," Thurman said.

Thurman's dedication to the people around him is evident, but his love for his own six children couldn't be stronger. "Everything I have done, from my church work to community work, has been involved with people. But even after doing all of that, my wife and I worked very, very hard to make sure our children were well taken care of." His voice boomed with pride as he relayed their success in education, careers, and family, blessing him with many grandchildren, great-grandchildren, and great-great-grandchildren.

Above all, Thurman delights the most in his children's relationships with Christ and their own desires to honor Him. "All my children have the same spirit I have, the spirit of giving and of loving people," he said. "We are a family of giving because we know what God has done for us. We know where it came from, and we know what He said in His Word."

Just as Thurman and his siblings observed everything their mother did, he and Hazel sought to model the lives they desire for their children. "We showed them, this is the way you love people, and this is the way you serve God."

Carried through Tragedy

The year 2000 brought tragedy to the Mitchells. Thurman's oldest son, Thurman Jr., was a former newscaster at KCTV5 and well known in the Kansas City community. He eventually left the station to become a pastor. On April 10, 2000, while preaching a sermon, Thurman Jr., had a stroke and passed away. He was fifty-five years old. "I couldn't believe or understand it," Thurman said. "It was devastating to me, just devastating."

In December of the same year, Thurman's beloved Hazel also passed away after fifty-eight years of marriage. "Those were two hard, hard blows," he said.

Within that same time span, Thurman lost seven people, including two brothers and a grandson. But through the pain, he never lost his love for his Savior. Thurman knows everything he has is a blessing from his heavenly Father. He knows what it means to have little, and he has been faithful with the material possessions he has had. Above all, Thurman has seen that true wealth is found in giving his life away to love people and serve God—in joy and in pain, in plenty and in want.

"Through all of that, I know God is real. I still love Him, and I'm going to trust Him and glorify Him," Thurman said. "He's my God and my Savior, and He has certainly brought me a very, very long way."

Surrounded by his family, Thurman went to be with his Savior on December 30, 2012. Hundreds attended his funeral, including the Wichita mayor, the chief of police, and many other civic leaders.

Your Story:

1. Is serving a trademark of your life? How can you develop a servant's heart?

2. Think about the spiritual mothers and fathers you have known. What about their lives influenced and inspired you? How do you want to model your life after theirs?

3. Are people a priority in your life? How do you use your home and your time to bless others?

4. In the face of tragedy or tough financial times, how do you react? Do you truly believe God to be a good and generous God?

CHAPTER THIRTEEN

Sending It Ahead

Andy Andreas

ANDY ANDREAS NEVER wanted to attend seminary, but when the Lord called him to Talbot School of Theology, he obeyed. Although Andy quickly realized he had neither the call nor the desire to be a pastor, it was clear the Lord had a purpose for his time in seminary. There, Andy soaked in God's truth and principles that would become the bedrock for his future in business.

"Through a series of events, a multimillionaire decided to pay for all of my seminary tuition," Andy said. "When someone is generous to you, you want to become generous as well. You want to be like that."

The Gift of Giving

Andy grew up surrounded by models of generosity. His mother always seemed to be sharing the gospel with someone at the kitchen table. He saw his dad's tithe envelope on the counter every week. He watched two of his dad's friends dedicate their businesses to God and show great generosity. These men were examples who helped set the vision for Andy's future business life.

Andy loved dropping change in the offering plate as a kid, and he was eager to give more. "When I got my very first paycheck, I couldn't wait to go to church and put my tithe in the offering. I had always wanted to do that from a very early age," Andy said. "In my case, I would say giving is a spiritual gift. I am energized by it. Some people are big on mercy or evangelism—it ignites them. I am a giver. I was just designed that way—and I love it."

Andy's life has taken many turns he never expected. He has a bachelor's degree in industrial technology and a master's in Bible and theology. He has been a salesman and a business owner. Today, he works in strategic development for the National Christian Foundation, where he combines his passion for business and ministry.

"I have learned you never want to hold tightly to the reins of your life because God has more things for you than you can ever conceive," he said. He's learned God is always out for your best, which is why he is so confident in letting go. "That is the Christian life. Surrender and it will be insane. It's a pretty simple equation—give God the reins to your life and see what He does. It's incomprehensible."

Yet, through all his vocations, Andy's vision for his life has never changed. He lives each day to fulfill his life's mission statement: *Andy Andreas exists to get as many people into heaven as he possibly can before he dies, and to have as much fun along the way as possible.* Whether it is hunting grizzly bears or other big game in Alaska, or perfecting a sales presentation, Andy lives life to its fullest.

God's Business

However, Andy knows following God's call can be challenging. Andy worked as a sales representative and manager for three years. But his life took another turn when his employer went out of business. As part of Andy's final paycheck, the company's owner gave Andy a copier, a fax machine, some desks, and a table saw.

With these new but limited resources, he felt God clearly leading him to start his own business. Andy didn't want to and asked God to change His mind. He told God, "You've got the wrong guy to start a business." Still, the call persisted. He knew he had to obey. "God owns me," Andy said. "I work for Him every day in whatever I'm doing. You can tell Him the truth—whatever you think and feel—but you still have to obey."

In faith, Andy started his own business, a bathroom remodeling company called Jubilee Home Solutions. "It wasn't fun at all," he recalled. "I went from making $123,000 a year as a sales rep to $13,000 that first year. The entire thing was a very growing experience. I was always pouring out my heart before God and asking Him for wisdom. I kept telling God that starting a business with me was a bad idea! But I remained obedient to God. It wasn't always easy, but it's been rewarding in so many ways."

> "You've got the wrong guy to start a business."

Andy decided the business should have the same purpose as his life: to bring people to Christ. With that mindset, he determined to use his company to fund the Great Commission. After about eighteen months, Andy and his partners figured out a solid business plan and everything began to take off. Jubilee grew and expanded to Denver, Minneapolis, and Dallas, and quickly became one of the largest bathroom remodeling companies in the country.

Giving Before Selling

As the business grew, it would have been easy to keep the profits. But for Andy, the math was simple: sell a remodeling job, reinvest in the company, and give to missions. For every remodeling job he sold, Andy saw another person who might go to heaven. For him, it was "Sell a toilet, save a soul."

Andy knew he wanted to give the profits of his business to God's Kingdom. And seven years after Andy obeyed God's call, Home Depot offered to buy the business. However, before he sold, God reminded Andy of a conversation he had with an attorney from the National Christian Foundation.

"I had lunch with this attorney about two years before all this happened, thank goodness, and I remembered him telling me you should give before you sell," Andy said. By giving stock in the company before he sold, Andy realized he could save substantially on taxes and thus be able to give more. In all, by giving stock before the sale, Andy saved millions of dollars.

However, when Andy asked God how much of the profit he should give, he received an answer he didn't like. God wanted 50 percent. Andy actually thought he should give more than 50 percent; he didn't want to keep the other half. "I talked to the Lord three times trying to get Him to change His mind and take more than 50 percent. For me, I realized I could focus on having a lot of 'stuff' in this life, or I could choose to defer my gain in this life and seek 'gain' in heaven. I want more in heaven!"

But once again, Andy obeyed. He set up a giving fund and put aside 50 percent of his company's value for Kingdom work. When his company sold, his giving fund received 50 percent of the sale proceeds. Then he began to give. He felt the Lord telling him to get rid of all the money in ten years.

"Disposing of all the money meant 'Get in there, get it going, and don't wait around.' My overarching philosophy is 'Give all you can give whenever you can give,'" Andy said. "When I think about investing, a good investment return might be 8 percent per year. But when I think about investing in God's Kingdom, I think of a thirty fold, sixty fold, or hundred times return—and I literally laugh as I write donation checks. I'm not sure, but I think that is the mindset of the hilarious giver in 2 Corinthians 9:7."

Handling God's Checkbook

When you have money to give, Andy believes it is vital to listen to God instead of being swayed by emotion or personal gain. When he has Kingdom investment opportunities presented to him, he finds that one of three things happens: (1) the Holy Spirit impresses him to give on the spot, (2) the Spirit says not to give, or (3) the Spirit tells him to pray and wait for an answer that will come later.

"The money is not yours; you just handle God's checkbook for Him. So when He says, 'Write that guy a check for this much,' you do it." Over the years, Andy has learned not to hide his gift of giving, but to use it strategically to inspire people. "Be cautiously open with it," he encouraged. "Not about

> "The money is not yours; you just handle God's checkbook for Him."

the amount, but with what generosity looks like, so it spurs others on toward love and good deeds."

For Andy, learning how Christians fit into God's economy sheds light on the call to generosity. He encourages other businessmen and women to make investments that will last for eternity. Andy said, "Kingdom ROI (return on investment) is incomprehensible. I like what Paul says in 1 Corinthians 2:9: 'But, as it is written, what no eye has seen, nor ear heard, nor the heart of man imagined, what God has prepared for those who love him.'"

"As Americans, we are the rich Christians in the world. If you have a business in the U.S., you're probably at the top one-tenth of 1 percent wage earners in the entire history of the world. We have one of the greatest opportunities to influence the spread of the gospel! What do you think Christ would have you do? My personal call as an American Christian is to be a giver because we have so much it's ridiculous," he said.

Today, Andy funds Bible translations and education for seminary students around the world. "I think the strategic nature of these opportunities is incredible. And it's funny how it worked out. There's a guy who pays for my tuition, and now the call of God on my life is to pay for seminary education for students in very strategic parts of the world. That guy gave me my seminary education, and God was able to lead me into multiplying it a hundred times," he said.

He concludes, "I'm a 'to-make-a-gain' guy, and I think most businesspeople are. If you want your work to count and not be completely lost, then send it ahead. That's where the real gain is."

Your Story:

1. Can you relate to Andy's desire to make a gain? How can you use your money or business to affect eternity and send it ahead?

2. How well are you handling God's checkbook? Can you think of a time God asked you to give and you obeyed?

3. God used a stranger's generosity to lead Andy to fund seminary students. Where have you experienced generosity in your life? Is God stirring your heart to give back?

CHAPTER FOURTEEN

Eternal Investments

Glen Scheib

A S THE PRESIDENT and CEO of his own small business, Glen Scheib had to trust God with each step in his company and in his giving. Glen grew up watching his parents give, often behind the scenes. Following their example, he and his wife, Gloria, have also committed to tithing. "We were making money, and as we got raises, it would disappear," Glen said. "We started tithing, and we ended up with more than what we had before. It is just a testimony to God's grace."

After establishing the pattern of tithing, Glen and Gloria have allowed God to increasingly lead them into the generous life. "As we stepped out in faith and God met us, we felt confident that we heard God's voice, so we kept giving as opportunities came around," Glen said. "It was and still is a growing process."

Steps of Faith

Glen founded Professional Accounting Services in 1980. He has trusted God with each investment and expansion, and he has experienced God's faithfulness as his business has grown. "It's a big deal for a small business to hire new employees," Glen said. "Time and time again we take the step to hire a new employee, and within two or three months, God has made up the difference. He has provided for us."

In one of his most remarkable stories, Glen sees God's provision a hundredfold. He had a family friend who started a new business making dog biscuits. As a new business, they did not have the capital to pay for accounting services. They asked Glen to provide the services for free until the business was making money. In return, they would give him shares in the business.

Glen was skeptical. He'd done other deals like this in the past, and his services usually went uncompensated. But Glen agreed to pray about it. To his surprise, he felt like God was leading him to provide the accounting services, so he obeyed.

During the first few years, Glen provided more than $30,000 worth of accounting services, and the deal didn't look so good. But just as with their early decision to give and to step out in faith, God did a funny thing. The dog biscuits began to sell like ... well, hotcakes. And with this rise in sales, the company grew in value, and so did Glen's shares.

In fact, the company grew so much that it began to attract the attention of much larger companies. As a potential sale loomed, Glen chose to take another step of faith. He gave away part of his shares. Glen realized that his gift of accounting services allowed him to make the corresponding gift of stock. When the company sold, Glen's initial gift of time had multiplied many times over for his family and for the Kingdom.

The Four P's

Glen desires to use God's resources in the best way possible, but he knows he is not perfect. "I would be lying if I said I did not make any mistakes in what I have done, whether it be investments or business decisions. It's a learning process."

Over the years Glen has learned to listen for God's voice, and he has discovered one way of making decisions. He calls it the Four P's:

Pray: First, Glen talks to God and asks Him to provide direction.

Plan: Glen begins to create a plan for his next gift or investment while continuing to pray about how God is leading him.

Plod: Next, he diligently and patiently works his plan.

Prosper: Glen decides beforehand how he will use his resources if God prospers his plan.

Looking for Fruit

Glen and Gloria are passionate about discipleship, and they tend to give to ministries with the same values. "It's exciting to be able to see someone who didn't know Christ not only saved, but on fire for the Lord and helping disciple others. There is nothing better than that," Glen said.

Glen has a God-given passion for business, and consequently, he likes to see results. Glen and his wife look for ministries that produce fruit before they invest God's money. "I am probably more selective in my giving than I once was. I am trying to be the best steward of what God has given me," Glen said. "To put it bluntly, I try to invest in those ministries that give God the biggest bang for His buck."

> "I try to invest in those ministries that give God the biggest bang for His buck."

Glen tries to be wise about his giving and at times, God allows him to see the fruits of his sacrifice. However, Glen admits, sometimes we won't know the outcome until heaven: "With a lot of ministries, you may never see the result. It may just be eternal rewards versus rewards we see now."

Living It Out

Glen believes generosity should touch all areas of life, not just his finances. In his family, that means passing on the love of giving to his children and grandchildren. In his business, living generously means providing good service to clients, spending time with his employees, and generating an others-focused culture by giving back to the community.

Glen would tell you living generously is a calling and doing it wisely is a process. He believes in the power of investing in an individual to change the world for Christ.

"I think there comes a point in everyone's life when you stop being the taker and become the giver," he said. "Try to invest in individuals whether it is through your time or your finances. Giving back is the key to Christian maturity. We quit living for ourselves and start living for others."

Your Story:

1. How do you decide when or where to give? For your next investment or gift, try using Glen's Four P's: Pray, Plan, Plod, and Prosper.

2. What are you passionate about? Make a list and circle at least three. Research ministries in your city and get involved either through volunteering or giving.

3. For Glen, generosity in his business means good service to clients, time with employees, and an others-focused culture. What does generosity look like in your workplace? How can you help foster it?

CHAPTER FIFTEEN

Sex, Money, and the Fight for Human Worth

Morgan Perry

IN A RED-LIGHT district in Thailand, a group of American students found a young girl lying on the side of the street. Completely naked and clearly drugged, the girl had been raped multiple times. Morgan was working with young prostitutes in Thailand, but this was her first personal encounter with a sex-trafficking victim, an issue that would quickly grip her heart.

"Before that encounter, I thought I was working with child and adult prostitutes. I didn't realize there was a huge illegal industry behind it," Morgan said. When confronted with this reality, she decided what her life should be dedicated to: "I wanted to expose this issue. Right then and there, at eighteen years of age, I was ready to do a documentary about sex trafficking."

Finding Direction

As she began to research the issue, Morgan learned 100,000 children are sexually exploited every day in the United States. At a minimum, these kids are forced to serve five customers per day.

"On the smallest scale of what we are looking at, that is half a million rapes of kids per day in America," Morgan said. "For some reason, this is floating under the radar. When people see the film and hear what's going on, they realize there is so much urgency around this issue. People are moved, and that has created a culture of generosity."

> "On the smallest scale of what we are looking at, that is half a million rapes of kids per day in America."

Morgan is choosing to listen to God's call for her even if it means giving up the typical life of a girl in her twenties. She, however, does not view her decision as a sacrifice: "This is the least I can do if I am looking at what Jesus did. It is so rewarding, and I am honored to be able to do it," she said.

Morgan grew up in a supportive family that loves Christ. She developed a passion for media as a little girl, and she could not wait to photograph the world for herself. As a kid, she dreamed of becoming a missionary, but high school brought rough times. "I got hit with some pretty hardcore life stuff and took a little detour from the Lord."

Morgan chose a college, but God had different plans for this aspiring photojournalist. "If I had gone to that university, I would probably be running a 'Save the Lemurs' campaign right now," Morgan laughed. "But the Lord intervened through my father; he wouldn't let me go to that school."

Instead, she decided to try Youth with a Mission, or YWAM, knowing her father would approve, and she would still get to travel. The Lord got Morgan's attention at a training session in New Zealand. "I had a revelation of who He is," she said. "So I took a leap of faith and recommitted my life to the Lord."

A God-sized Issue

Morgan went on to study photojournalism with the University of the Nations through YWAM. Through her experience in Thailand and studying in more than thirty countries, she saw a theme of sex trafficking. She and her fellow photojournalists began processing all they had learned and decided to publish a book, *Sex and Money: A Global Search for Human Worth*.

While researching the book, Morgan's team first discovered the grave status of sex trafficking in the United States through a podcast. "The pastor shared a story about a girl who was held in a dog cage and prostituted for about forty days before she was rescued," Morgan said. "She was forced to have sex about fifteen to twenty times per day—and this was in Arizona. At this point, I had studied all international issues and never focused on America. So I started digging it up more. America only makes up 5 percent of the world population, but we're driving 25 percent of child sex tourism worldwide."

Once Morgan's team decided to focus their efforts in America, Morgan watched God bless the project. For two years, Morgan and her core team worked on developing the documentary, *Sex and Money: A National Search for Human Worth*, as they traveled to thirty states, and conducted seventy-five interviews with survivors of trafficking, politicians, experts in the field, porn stars, and many more, all while living in a thirty-two-foot RV. But to fund this project, Morgan and her team had to raise a lot of money. She wondered if anyone would give significant dollars to a twenty-one-year-old girl.

Cultivating Generosity

Morgan learned to trust God as she watched Him provide for the film time and time again. She said, "When we give our lives to a cause, God is honored. If anything, I think God smiles on those who are willing to give selflessly to Him." At the same time, it still takes faith.

"A week before the first week of filming, we had no money. I had never raised more than $5 from a lemonade stand," Morgan said. "I was so discouraged."

The next day, Morgan joined a conference call with a potential giver. Within twenty minutes of explaining the project, the donor gave $20,000, allowing Morgan's team to begin production.

"Every time I've hit a low, the Lord has always provided, and it has always been beyond me," she said. "It has turned into a culture of generosity; there is a whole movement behind it."

Before long, the film became a $1.2 million project as people donated money, camera equipment, and volunteer hours. The majority of the budget was covered through gifts in kind and donated services. Most of the campaign staff and film crew were comprised of YWAM missionaries and college interns from all over the country who donated their time. This incredible generosity allowed Morgan's team to develop a fifty-state awareness campaign to accompany the film.

"People were so moved by the issue and so ready to sacrifice," Morgan said. "People just kept giving. It has changed our lives as we've seen people give."

The Hands of Christ

Morgan could be doing any variety of things in her twenties, but she is choosing to dedicate her life to serving the Lord and loving trafficking victims. God has shown Morgan and her team that love equals sacrifice. By all rights, Morgan should be pursuing corporate jobs and endeavors that would be easier and, more rewarding financially.

"There are so many things that naturally I would rather be doing. I am more introverted, and, financially speaking, it is definitely a challenge," she said. "To love these girls, we have to sacrifice a lot so we can make this movie. To love our King, we have to sacrifice a lot so we can live in community."

Morgan's film crew lives by this mantra: *Intimacy unto advocacy*. They are committed to seeking a personal relationship with God before fighting for their cause. This belief is anchored in Matthew 22:36–40, where Jesus gives the first and second commandment (love God and love others). They believe God put the commandments in that order because loving God first equips them to be effective advocates for others.

"Justice causes these days are very trendy, and everyone in our generation cares about everything," Morgan said. "No matter how big the vision gets, how bad the issue is, how many people you're trying to help, if at the end of the day loving the Lord isn't first—if you're loving your ministry

> "If at the end of the day loving the Lord isn't first ... that defeats the purpose of everything."

over Him, or you're loving people over Him—that defeats the purpose of everything."

Everything comes back to God and the individual. Sex trafficking is a staggering issue, but Morgan knows God wants her to befriend victims on a personal level. One young girl shared her horrific story with Morgan's film crew. The girl ran away from home, was kidnapped in San Diego, and trafficked to Mexico. She escaped once and was raped by the police as she tried to reach the border. She escaped another time and was raped again before getting swept back into trafficking.

"This little girl, she is so beautiful, and she was sex trafficked in all the ways it is defined," Morgan said. "When she finished her story, the director of the film asked her, 'What did your friends say when you came back?' She looked at him so quickly and said, 'Oh, I don't have any friends.' That is the problem. If this girl had community, if she had fellowship, if she had friends, then she would never have run away from home, and this never would have happened. It's all back to the one person. One child at a time, one friend at a time. That's what it means to be the hands of Christ with this issue."

Your Story:

1. God's heart breaks over such injustices as sex trafficking. Is He calling you to get involved with this issue? How can you contribute?

2. God is using Morgan's passion for media to significantly affect sex trafficking. What are your gifts and passions? How can you use them generously for God?

3. Does your relationship with God take priority over your work, ministry, and relationships? If not, what needs to change?

4. Morgan and her team realized it is really about the one person. Think about the people in your life who are hurting. Who is God asking you to minister to? What could that look like even this week?

CHAPTER SIXTEEN

Triple Capital

Pete & Debbie Ochs

WHEN PETE OCHS had the chance to sell his business, he and his wife, Debbie, recognized an incredible giving opportunity. Debbie encouraged Pete to sell the business so they could use the money to fund a ministry project they had been working on for several years. Pete agreed and sold the business just as the healthcare industry fell on rough times.

"We closed the deal, funded the ministry, and nine months later, the company who bought us filed for bankruptcy, as did most of the companies in that industry," Pete said. Pete knew God provided the funds for the school and protected them from financial hardship. That instance made a deep impression on Pete: God is in control. Since then, Pete has worked diligently to steward God's resources well.

Growing Generosity

Pete watched his parents model generosity growing up. One Christmas, Pete discovered a new red wagon hidden at his house. Assuming it was his present, he waited anxiously for the big day. On Christmas Eve, Pete's dad took the family on a special errand. They pulled up in front of a stranger's house, and to Pete's dismay, his dad retrieved the red wagon, filled with an assortment of toys, from their car. "I couldn't believe it, but we pulled that wagon into this very poor family's house, and those kids went crazy," Pete recalled. "I was blessed at an early age to see very generous, giving parents."

Pete pursued a degree in business and willingly gave what he thought God required. "I was a 90/10 guy; 10 percent for God, 90 for me. I wanted to make a lot of money so my 10 percent would be big," Pete laughed.

> "I was a 90/10 guy; 10 percent for God, 90 for me."

When Pete was thirty years old, he took a Crown Financial Ministries course that shifted his perspective on possessions and business. God used that class to bring stewardship into clear focus for Pete.

"I understood from that day forward that God owned it all and I was just the manager," he said. "That really started my giving journey. That started to change the way I did business." Today, Pete understands the excitement of giving: "It just gives me great joy to give," he said. "Probably one of the most fun things I do is to write checks we give away."

Pete and Debbie have passed their love of giving to their children. Once a year, they gather with their two children and spouses for a family meeting. They discuss the fruit from their giving in the last year, and then they begin to plan for the future. "As a family, we figure out how much money we want to give away, and then we talk about various ministries we want to support," Pete said. "To see the impact on them is amazing because they now have a generous spirit that I never had."

The Bottom Line

On the business side of things, whether it's real estate, manufacturing, healthcare, or hydroelectricity, Pete has a big vision for his ventures. Pete is the president of Capital III, Inc., a private equity investment company. The "III" stands for a triple bottom line.

"We want to generate economic capital for the benefit of our employees, customers, and stakeholders. We want to create social capital that forges strong relationships inside the family, church, business, and community. And we want to create spiritual capital. Spiritual capital is people—whether they are customers, vendors, or employees—coming to know Christ," he said.

In the business of business, Pete has experienced many ups and downs. It can be hard to give when profits are low, but Pete has learned God is ultimately in control. "It is easy for me to give out of my excess or surplus, but true generosity is if I continue to give even though I don't have excess. That's probably the true test of faith."

Pete also struggles with the tension between either reinvesting profits to grow his businesses or giving the money away. "That is the conundrum for me as a business guy," he said. "I really try to ask God often what He wants me to do today or this week." Pete consistently takes questions before the Lord and tries to grow in sensitivity toward His leading. When things still seem unclear, Pete leans toward generosity. "I would always err on the side of giving versus investing."

Giving LIFE

Pete has a heart for start-up ministries, and he desires to see them flourish. "Oftentimes in ministry, if you can be the first guy in—the guy to get the momentum going—then other people get on the bandwagon," he said. "I like being that entrepreneurial pioneer, first-guy-in, because I think it leverages your giving dollars."

> "I like being that entrepreneurial pioneer, first-guy-in, because I think it leverages your giving dollars."

Pete and Debbie believe in partnering with ministries beyond giving financially, and they seek to give LIFE. "If you are going to be generous, you should be generous with your LIFE," Pete said. "LIFE is an acrostic for Labor, Influence, Finance, and Expertise. To the people we give the largest amounts of money, not only do we give our finances, but we try to give our labor, our influence, and our expertise."

Pete and Debbie met through Young Life, and they continue to serve on committees or as volunteer leaders for that ministry. While Pete said they give consistently to a few organizations, he has also grown in spontaneous generosity.

"I have typically viewed all of my giving from a very planned, strategic perspective, which I don't think is wrong, but I think sometimes I miss some blessings by not being more spontaneous," he said. Debbie attended a Generous Giving Conference where she heard a speaker talk about spontaneous giving.

"The next week, we had the opportunity to be really spontaneous and really bless somebody," Pete said. "It was out of the ordinary for us, but we did it." They watched their gift increase faith in people who had been praying for that need to be met. "The blessings we have seen come out of that were phenomenal," Pete said.

Time and time again God has used generosity to show Pete that He is in control. "Because I'm a business guy and we're in business to make money, I can be a man of really little faith; I want to figure it out on my own," Pete said. "The biggest thing generosity has done for me is expand my faith and allow me to see how God has worked in spite of me."

Your Story:

1. Do you tend to be strategic or spontaneous in your giving? Seek specific disciplines to help you grow in your weaker giving style.

2. When money is tight, how much of a priority is giving in your life?

3. Where are you committing your Labor, Influence, Finances, and Expertise? If you're not, what would it look like to give your LIFE to a specific ministry?

4. How are you seeking spiritual capital through your work? Do you seek to build Christ-centered relationships with your clients, employees, and coworkers?

CHAPTER SEVENTEEN

An Atheist Finds Freedom

Craig Miller

LOOKING OUT HIS office window one day, Craig Miller began to evaluate his life. Craig was in his late twenties and already living his dream life—or so he thought. His colleagues viewed him as a guy who got what he wanted in life; however, he was miserable on the inside. "I was a young guy making a six-figure income and buying the things I thought would make me happy and the things I thought would make me look successful," Craig said. "I came to the place where I realized even if I had Michael Jordan's money, I wouldn't be happy."

That day, he got up from his desk and walked across the street into the nearest church. He didn't have a plan, but he had a vague inclination he might find what he had been missing. As a fourth-generation atheist, Craig was raised with a skeptical view of Christians, seeing religion as a "crutch" for the weak. After wandering around the church, a lady asked him if he was lost. "I suppose I probably am," Craig replied. She directed him to a pastor, and Craig sat down to talk with him. The Holy Spirit worked through the pastor as he began to address Craig's unspoken judgments and doubts.

"Christianity is not a crutch; it's a strength," the pastor said. Craig recalled his feelings as the pastor spoke, "I had an immediate sense that I was hearing the truth and an immediate sense that I was having my thirst quenched." Craig began to attend church, moving up in the pews each week as an insatiable hunger for the Word of God grew within him.

"Finally, when I really understood God's grace and love and understood what had been done for me and how much He loved me, I fell on my face and really gave my life to Christ."

Learning Lordship—Letting Go of Career

A major step in Craig's journey toward the generous Christian life began with realizing everything belongs to God. "He is allowing me to be in charge of these things He has entrusted me with," Craig said. "At minimum, I need to be obedient to what He has taught in His Word. At best, I need to completely, with abandon, trust Him and be willing to give beyond what might seem rational to me."

For Craig, senior vice president of First Trust Mortgage, his first task was to lay his career at God's feet. Craig surrendered the temptation to do what might benefit him most and dedicated himself to honoring God with how he conducted business.

"In the mortgage industry, we have a lot of greed. A lot of bad things have come from poor business practices and not taking care of consumers the way they should be," Craig said. "I had to remember every time: This is God's money. If I refinance someone's home, He'll own all of it. How would He want me to do it? What's the right thing? My business has been blessed because I turned it over to Him, not because I'm such a smart business man."

As he began to walk with Christ, God gave Craig a new heart for helping people. He often goes beyond what is expected in his industry to teach others about wise financial planning. "It has been a ministry to help people realize God owns it all," he said.

Craig used to think he needed to travel overseas to share the gospel, but God has revealed to him the mission field in his office building. "I have so many people who come to me in a vulnerable position because they are concerned about their finances," Craig said. "I have a ton of opportunities to witness to people for Christ and even edify Christians who are strong believers but need to be reminded of God's principles."

From a Shotgun to a Spear

Early on, Craig found himself "shot-gunning" money wherever it was needed. Whether someone wanted to sell him a raffle ticket, a candy bar, or asked for thousands of dollars for a charity event, Craig was eager and willing to give. "I was giving to anyone who came to me because they heard they could get money. I felt like I was doing the right thing because I was helping them, and I had an abundance that wasn't mine to keep," he said.

God began to redirect his giving from "shot-gunning" to what Craig calls "throwing a spear." "Now, my heart is for the Word of God and people being saved by Christ. Period." With this new focus, Craig is wiser about how he gives. He does his research and prays about where God wants his money to go. Through this approach, he has seen his giving make a more significant impact than when he scattered his resources.

> "God began to redirect his giving from 'shot-gunning' to what Craig calls 'throwing a spear.'"

However, Craig admits it's possible to take strategic giving too far. Sometimes you just have to let it go. "I think a lot of people are hesitant to give because they don't know what the fruit of it will be," he said. "What I am finding now is that if there is a cause I believe will truly glorify God and lead people to Christ, I can trust God with the outcome of what will happen with that money."

Starting His Own Legacy

With no previous heritage of faith in his family, Craig has become passionate about passing on generosity. Craig has blatantly challenged his coworkers to be generous and reminded them where their success comes from. "I would have meetings with my staff and say, 'God has inspired us to do business the right way. All we are doing is the right thing, and we are reaping a huge harvest. If you are not giving back like you should and you are not trusting God, you're not going to be free.'"

Craig's biggest passion is teaching his children to be generous. He is constantly looking for new lessons, whether it is helping someone push a broken-down car or paying for a random family's meal at a restaurant. "I'm not doing it to get the admiration of my kids, but I do want them to be people of action when they grow up. When they see a need, they jump on it; they don't ponder whether or not they can be of assistance," Craig said.

Finding Freedom

Although God has clearly given Craig a passion for generosity, it is not always easy. Craig has faced opposition from people who think his giving is excessive or irrational. At the same time, he has dealt with his own temptations to be prideful.

As an example, one of the things he personally wrestled with is a love for cars. He had an eye for classic cars and accumulated quite a collection. But God began dealing with him on these issues. Craig understands the desire to use stuff to obtain happiness, but he has seen it ultimately leads to disappointment.

"I had all the things that most people see as their goals in life at an early enough age to realize that it will never amount to anything of great value," Craig said. "No matter what you think that money will give you, it will never give you nearly as much as what you will get from giving it away. You will never feel the same way about it."

> "Think about it … a vehicle bought freedom."

As part of his learning, Craig began to give away his vehicles. One of the last vehicles he gave away was a 1966 show-quality vehicle. When the vehicle was sold, he gave the proceeds to a ministry that works with sex-trafficking victims. "Think about it … a vehicle brought freedom. Our stuff can be given away to bring about the liberty of others."

For Craig, generosity equals freedom. Freedom from accumulation of stuff. Freedom from self-recognition. Freedom to live and enjoy fellowship with his Creator.

Your Story:

1. Can you relate to Craig's story? Have you ever obtained something you thought would make you happy just to discover it wouldn't satisfy?

2. What is holding you captive? Is it money, success, possessions, other people's opinions, your own pride, etc.?

3. Are you "shot-gunning" or "throwing a spear" with your giving? Is it effective for God's Kingdom?

4. Do you see generosity as a burden or as freeing? Ask God to change your perspective on giving from an obligation to a joy. Remember, He already owns it all—He's asking for your obedience and your heart.

CHAPTER EIGHTEEN

Micro-Finance and Macro-Change

Gary & Jan Venable

INSTEAD OF GIVING him the whole picture at once, God led Gary Venable into generosity one step at a time. As Gary and his wife, Jan, have stepped into greater obedience, they have seen the ripple effect generosity has on themselves and others.

Gary, CEO at All Systems Designed Solutions, Inc., first discovered his passion for India during short-term mission trips. The Venables have since helped establish businesses, churches, and Christian schools in Hindu villages.

"I recognized the poverty of Christians in India and the crippling effect of their total dependence on outside financial help for their churches, and I wanted to help them," Gary said.

Specifically, Gary and Jan wanted to start a Christian school that would be financially self-sustaining. "God cast a vision in our hearts of things that could be accomplished, but they couldn't be accomplished without significant financial resources."

As God called Gary and Jan into this vision, they knew they didn't have a significant lump sum of money. But God opened up a series of events that made the path clear. First, they attended a Generous Giving Conference, where they learned about giving at levels they had not previously dreamed about, including giving of their assets. Second, they began meeting with strong charitable giving advisors.

They also learned they could create a giving fund where they could make annual contributions to the fund. Within a few years, Gary and Jan had a sizeable account they could begin using to fund the adventure they believed God was calling them to embark upon.

"When I look back, I can't imagine that I would have even agreed to take the first step if I had realized what the last step would look like. But God doesn't ask us to do that. He just asks us to be obedient, so we were," he said. "Because of that, there are dozens of new churches, multiple Christian schools, and some businesses—all of which are influencing the Christian community in India."

Self-Sustaining Work

Gary has a desire to see the Great Commission fulfilled in India. Giving micro-loans is one way he and Jan hope to accomplish God's work. They have learned that even small gifts can greatly influence someone for God's Kingdom.

For one woman, leaving Hinduism to follow Christ came at a great cost. Her husband abandoned her, leaving her desolate and with little possibility of finding work. A micro-loan allowed her to buy and raise a pig for income. She then had enough money to earn a living by trading cloth with women in surrounding villages.

"We think the need is too great, that we hardly make a difference here," Jan said. "But God can make a huge difference by our willingness."

Gary added, "And that was just a tiny, tiny piece of the money."

> "But God can make a huge difference by our willingness."

Micro-finance opportunities have transformed people's lives like Mohan, an Indian pastor, who receives income from a water buffalo he was able to buy, or Anapaum, who uses the money from his chicken farm to expand the small orphanage he runs.

Gary and Jan have also helped fund the Christian schools in India they first dreamed about. These schools teach Scripture and

Christian songs as a part of the English curriculum and help believers connect with Hindu families in the village. "I recognized Christian schools were a way to help develop self-sustaining ministries, as well as evangelize and connect with lost people and lost families," Gary said.

One school, Immanuel International Academy, was designed to reach middle class students with quality education and the knowledge of Christ. "Ultimately, it will influence hundreds of students and their families as well as earn money for the Kingdom projects there," Gary said.

A Difficult Task

Although the Venables have seen God use their efforts, they have often encountered opposition while pursuing their mission. "All these visions of what you want to accomplish sound great and look great strategically, but actually implementing them and getting the work done is very frustrating, time-consuming, and difficult," Gary said.

Gary has to wade through many differences in culture and business in India. He knows that Satan wants to exploit those frustrations to inhibit Kingdom gain.

"All of their processes are different; they think differently, and they don't always understand what we are trying to accomplish. I suspect we frustrate them as much as they frustrate us," he said. "It's something we always have to guard against: not letting Satan get in the way of achieving the vision God gives."

Sometimes, Gary does not see the fruit of his work right away. During one of his trips, his team established a church in a village but left without seeing many people reached for Christ. "I was disappointed. I just assumed Satan was winning out," Gary said. Gary may have assumed defeat, but God wasn't finished. About three months later, Gary received a report that a small fellowship of believers had been established in that same village.

God has continued to reveal His heart to the Venables. Jan's first trip to India was a stretching experience for her, but the Lord used it to transform her life. "I knew it would really affect me—the poverty, the difference in culture, and everything else," Jan said. "But I think once you go to a foreign country, it's really the people that touch you. These are sweet, wonderful, caring individuals who haven't had the same opportunities we have. Being with the people really changed me. You still see the poverty, but the loving eyes, the children, had a huge effect on me."

Generosity Near and Far

While they have given many resources to their work in India, the Venables are just as passionate about generosity at home. They enjoy helping their family grasp the joy of giving as well as meeting needs in their own community. They have encouraged their children and ten grandchildren to give generously. Each year they give their grandchildren money to decide for themselves where they want to give.

"You never know what the Lord will do with our family giving fund, whether it will be gone or still here when we pass on, so ultimately we want our children and our grandchildren to know how to handle it as well as their personal incomes and wealth," Gary said.

The Venables give to their church and also enjoy supporting kids going to camp, youth participating in leadership conferences or mission trips, and families in full-time ministry. However, the Venables don't give to everything.

"First and foremost as a believer, we want to be giving in ways that advance the Kingdom," Gary said. "There are a lot of what I call 'social-do-good opportunities' out there, but they are not Christ-centered."

Gary has learned that God is at work everywhere, and it doesn't take much searching to join His call to generosity. "If He is telling you to give locally, there are plenty of opportunities here to advance the Kingdom. If He is telling you to do it in India, China, Canada, or Europe, there are plenty of opportunities. You just have to seek what He is telling you."

> "It doesn't take much searching to join God's call to generosity."

Your Story:

1. God doesn't usually show us the entire picture at once. Like the Venables, are you trusting God with your giving by taking one step of obedience at a time?

2. Even when you can't see the fruit of your giving, do you believe God will finish His work? How can you remind yourself of God's faithfulness even when you're discouraged?

3. The Venables have seen how a seemingly small gift can greatly influence one person's life. What is one way you can make a difference in someone's life this week?

CHAPTER NINETEEN

Discovering the Joy

Frank Brown

W HEN HE HANDS strangers a $50 bill, some cry, others hug and thank him in disbelief, but Frank Brown just smiles and tells them to thank Jesus. It's His money. Frank has a vibrant passion for generosity. Giving invigorates him and brings him great joy. As Frank has become more of a strategic giver over the years, he still chooses to keep $50 in his wallet to give away—just for fun.

"If you're looking for someone who might be helped or blessed by it, then you are aware of people around you," Frank said. "What I think matters more to the recipient than the $50 is they feel like God knows their needs, knows they're alive, and did something to touch them."

Jesus, Jeans, and Guitars

Frank wasn't always joyfully generous. His parents divorced when he was ten years old, and his father raised him without a Christian influence. After Frank got married, he primarily went to church to please his wife, Barbara. "It felt good, but it didn't mean a whole lot," he said. "We rocked along for years that way."

The Browns moved to Kansas City in 1964, but they couldn't settle on a new church. Frank was working as a commercial airline pilot, and his constant travel strained their family. "Church was one of the issues we were unhappy about, so that seemed like an easy thing to solve. Just stop going," Frank recalled.

In 1971, Frank's fifteen-year-old daughter started attending Jesus Kids' gatherings multiple times a week. Frank was perplexed that church could be so exciting to a teenager, so he and his wife went to check out the meetings. "There was a hippie-looking kid who would pick up all these neighborhood teenagers and take them off. We went, and it was a mind-boggling thing for me."

Frank found four hundred kids sitting on the floor of a church basement wearing jeans and praising God with guitars. The scene made him feel uncomfortable and old-fashioned. He had considered himself a Christian for years, but he didn't understand the personal relationship with Christ this group talked about.

"From a worldly sense, everything in my life was going great," Frank said. "I had a dream job as an airline pilot, a beautiful wife, and four kids. I lived in a really pretty place; I had good health; I was making good money ... you name it. Everything was going well, but I was restless and dissatisfied."

Frank's daughter continued to pray for him, and eventually one speaker helped Frank navigate through his questions. Frank began walking with Christ and has now followed Him for more than forty years. "It hasn't been easy," he said. "I had to do a lot of changing, and I'm still a work in process."

A World of Opportunity

When Frank became a Christian he also became a faithful tither, though what that looks like has changed over the years. Frank started a bank courier business with his son and son-in-law as a side hobby. After twenty-five years as a pilot, Frank retired to focus on the bank business and to spend more time with his wife, who battled cancer for more than thirteen years. When she passed away, Frank found himself at a new stage in his life and his giving.

"At that point I had airline retirement; I had social security; I had a profitable business; I had investments; my kids were grown and doing well; and their future looked secure," Frank said. "It was not hard to figure out. I had always known that God had a purpose for the reason He was blessing me financially."

> "I had always known that God has a purpose for the reason He was blessing me financially."

Frank determined to use his resources for God, but he didn't know where to start. When an attorney pointed him toward the National Christian Foundation, the possibilities began to fall into place. "When I saw the tools and options that the foundation offered, the light bulb went on. Here's how I could do what I think God would have me to do with what He has given me," Frank said.

Frank took advantage of the foundation's ability to handle non-cash gifts. When he was ready to transfer ownership of his business to his son, NCF helped him do so in a way that benefited God's Kingdom and saved him a lot of taxes. Over a period of six years, Frank donated shares of the company to the foundation and his son bought them back. The money from the transfer went into a giving fund with the foundation, which Frank used to give to ministries.

Frank also learned how to gift his land strategically, and he donated one of his farms to NCF as undeveloped property. He then bought it back from the foundation through a limited liability corporation, or LLC. He donated 100 percent ownership in the LLC to the foundation, and he became the manager.

"I proceeded to develop a subdivision, put in roads, put in utilities, and started selling lots," Frank explained. "When it's all sold, it will be worth about $650,000. So what was a $200,000 asset—factoring in $200,000 in expenses—will end up being worth more than $400,000 for the Kingdom. It's an example of what a business guy can do if he is willing to put a little time and effort into it."

> "It's an example of what a business guy can do if he is willing to put a little time and effort in it."

With money available for the Kingdom, the joy of giving quickly became a reality for Frank. He has never looked back.

"Being involved with a foundation opened up the world to me as far as what God is doing," he said. "Early on I was like a drunken sailor—I was giving to anyone and everyone, and it was a lot of fun."

Since then, Frank has grown in giving wisely and strategically. He gives to fewer ministries, choosing to focus on ones with big visions and strong leadership. But as the $50 bills show, he still enjoys giving spontaneously.

"There are two things you should experience from giving," Frank said. "You should experience the joy of giving. It's really fun, which is counter-intuitive because we think it would be more fun to spend money or accumulate it. And two, you should feel like you accomplish something."

To accomplish work for the Kingdom, Frank believes donors need to know the people in a ministry and get involved beyond writing a check.

Helping Others Hear

Frank is passionate about God's Word and has partnered with ministries like Faith Comes By Hearing, an organization dedicated to translating and recording the Bible in the heart languages of people around the world. He has also supported SCPX(the Student Church Planting Experience), a movement that trains student leaders to start simple churches on dorm floors across the nation.

Frank has led his family into generosity as well. He opened a giving fund through NCF and let his teenage grandchildren give the money away. "The goal, of course, is that they will all experience the joy of giving," he said.

Throughout his journey in generosity, Frank has noticed a startling incongruity: Americans have extraordinary resources, but ministries are always strapped for funding. Frank encourages ministries and donors to consider themselves partners in God's work.

"There's a disconnect. God's people have an overwhelming, exceeding abundance of funding, and they're sitting on it when there are all these needs," Frank said. "I think in our hearts, because we are made in God's image, we have a desire to be generous, to do something worthwhile with what we have. However, we often don't know what to do, just like me for all those years."

God has transformed Frank from a strict tither to a blissfully generous giver, and he enjoys helping others make the same journey. "Out of being obedient to giving, my whole spiritual life has been invigorated, upgraded, and ramped up," he said. Frank continues to discover the joy in giving, and he can't wait for the next stranger to receive an unexpected blessing from God.

Your Story:

1. Have you discovered the joy in giving? If not, what's holding you back? If so, how can you use your story to help others also experience joy?

2. Where is most of your wealth? Pray about ways you can use your possessions for God's Kingdom.

3. Why do you think there is a disconnect between the wealth of Christians and the financial needs of ministries? Maybe you can make an impact by living more generously, by inspiring others, or by connecting donors with the right ministries. What role is God calling you to?

4. Frank believes donors should know the people in ministry and get involved in the organization beyond writing a check. How can you get involved with a ministry?

CHAPTER TWENTY

The First Yes

Barb May

T HE FIRST STEP toward your next adventure often begins with saying yes.

Barb May has worked in the financial services industry for twenty-five years, and her husband, Joe, is an insurance broker. While they enjoyed giving, they never considered themselves much of a story because they were not able to give at a high level. However, what started as a Christmas experiment has changed the way their family views giving.

A Christmas Yes

In 2008, Joe and Barb began discussing their Christmas shopping list. Their combined families included eleven children, twenty-one grandchildren, and six great-grandchildren. Although they enjoyed finding, wrapping, and exchanging gifts, they realized the gifts themselves were really not that significant. Their entire family, including Joe and Barb, had jobs and thus did not need the gifts purchased for them.

Joe and Barb posed the question to their family: Is there a better way to use the money normally spent on Christmas gifts? The family responded, "Yes! Let's do something different about Christmas. We'll have a white elephant exchange on Christmas Day and the money we've saved on gifts can be given away."

> "Yes! Let's do something different about Christmas."

Little did they know that this "yes" would be the first step in a family giving adventure.

Do Something Different

Several years later, in 2010, Barb felt a nudge to do something else different, maybe get involved with a ministry that spoke to her heart. Around this same time, she received an invitation to a "coffee and meet" with The GO Project, a global orphan care ministry.

This meeting led to an introduction to Marsha Campbell, a GO staff member, and to an invitation to travel to Haiti on a vision trip. Barb and Marsha's first lunch was two-and-a-half hours long with words gusting to six hundred per minute as they described their hopes and hearts for this next adventure.

Barb said yes to the vision trip invitation and joined Marsha and a team of sixteen on a trip to Haiti in March 2011.

However, once Barb reached Haiti, she wanted to curl up in her hotel bed with a blanket over her head. It had been a little over a year since the devastating Haiti earthquake, and the poverty and destruction were still so evident. As their team drove through the streets in their little white GO bus, they would just sit and let the tears come. Clouds of hazy dust from vehicles filled the air as pigs trotted through food lying on the streets of tent villages constructed among the rubble.

That first night, Barb told one of her friends, "I will never come back. It is just too hard to look at all this."

A Boy and a Ball

The next day, they were scheduled to visit one of the GO orphan villages. Barb said, "As we were disembarking from our bus, I noticed a small boy, maybe six years old, standing away from the other children. I had a tennis ball in my hand, so I tossed it to him. We stood there for a long time without saying anything, just tossing the ball back and forth and playing catch." After awhile, the boy stopped and leaned back against a tent pole. He smiled and said, "Photo, photo." Barb pulled out her camera and took his picture.

After the picture was taken, the boy reached for Barb's hand and wordlessly led her to a bench under the tent. This tent, or the tattered remains of it, served as the school and church since the original building had been destroyed in the earthquake.

Barb said, "He motioned for me to sit down on the bench. Then, he crawled up into my lap, put both arms around my neck, and just tunneled in. I just sat there and held him for a long time. I couldn't speak his language; he couldn't speak mine, so the only thing I knew to do was pray with him. I folded my hands and looked at him. He nodded yes, so I prayed for this sweet orphan child."

That night, Barb told her friend that she knew she wanted to go somewhere and serve orphans, but she definitely did not want to come back to Haiti, not someplace where it hurt like this.

Now What?

Near the end of the trip, Barb's group was invited to meet a women's group from a Haitian church. These women were responsible for making sure each orphan at their church had a bath and clean, ironed clothes on Saturday nights before church. Through an interpreter, each woman stood up, introduced herself, and explained a little about her family.

Barb said, "Although the women did not have physical things to give, they gave what they could—their beautiful, generous spirits. And even though they did not speak the same language as our group, we connected through being women and loving the same things—family and home."

On the plane back to the United States, Barb told her friend, "I want to come back to Haiti, and I'm already excited about my next trip!"

However, once Barb was back home, she had to decide what to do next. Each evening in Haiti, their team had gathered to pray, share thoughts, ask questions, and further explore the experience. During the last evening, the challenge was, "Now that you've seen, now that you know, what are you going to do about it?" Barb said, "I wanted and needed to say yes, but how, and to what?"

God's Invitation

The first part of the answer came when Barb was invited to celebrate with Marsha and a group of her friends who were working with a local school in Uganda. At this party, Barb heard about a new project: GO wanted to build an orphan village in Rukore, Uganda, a village in the mountains near the Rwandan border. The needs list included a variety of items and cost amounts. However, the top dollar item was the construction of the actual home. After reviewing the list, Barb and Joe said yes to the project, but weren't sure at what level they could participate.

Around this same time, Barb received a letter from an attorney regarding an inheritance from her uncle and aunt, Harry and Ann Ohlendorf. Barb had many fond memories of Harry and Ann because they loved all their nieces and nephews even though they never had children of their own. Barb was grateful they thought of her, but she went to the bank expecting a small amount, maybe a thousand dollars at most. However, when Barb saw the amount left for her, she was in shock. She shared the news with Joe and he immediately said, "Well, we just got your answer! We're building a house in Uganda."

> "We just got your answer! We're building a house in Uganda."

After combining it with funds they would have spent on Christmas, and with some of their savings, the inheritance money provided just enough to let the Mays build the house in Uganda and support nine children and a local mama for three years. Joe said, "What better tribute could we give to Barb's aunt and uncle—two wonderful people who loved children, but didn't have their own—than to provide a home for children who have no parents."

Christmases Now

As the years go by, Barb and Joe have continued to provide opportunities to do Christmas different. For Christmas 2012, and the next two years, the money that would have gone toward Christmas gifts has provided for children in the Rukore house in Uganda.

Since the time Joe and Barb said yes to doing Christmas different, their family has also provided a room for a family at the Salvation Army Family Lodge in Kansas and has built a well in an African village.

One favorite year was a "Pay It Forward" Christmas where every family member (even the smallest) receiving a signed check, amount filled in, but payee blank. Their only requirement was to give it to someone who needed it more. Many good stories came out of this, but the one Barb loves most is from a three-year-old great-grandson. He cashed his check for coins so he could hear the money drop in the Salvation Army bucket.

Going Back ... with Grandchildren

In November 2012, Joe and Barb returned to Haiti on another vision trip. But this time, two of their sixteen-year-old grandchildren said yes to the invitation to join them.

Barb worried that the culture shock and the long days might be too much for teenagers accustomed to an affluent American suburb. In particular, one day they had an hours-long bus ride up a mountain to visit a remote orphan village where several doctors from the States were examining the children. Barb thought surely her grandchildren must be bored and wondering why their grandmother had dragged them on this trip.

However, once they finally reached the orphan village, her grandson stopped her and said, "Thank you so much for bringing me. I want to become a doctor and do what these doctors are doing for these kids."

Barb's granddaughter added, "I didn't really know why we did Christmas different until now. But now I understand."

Barb said, "It has been such a blessing to see how our giving experience has already had a huge impact on our family ... and all because we started saying yes."

Your Story:

1. It can be tempting to assume we must wait for an inheritance or a better job before we can give enough to make a difference. However, where might God be calling you to say yes now?

2. As you think about your giving journey, what stories have specifically changed you? For Barb, it was a little orphan boy who wanted to be held. What are those stories for you? And where are you giving because of them?

3. As you consider Joe and Barb's family commitment to "do Christmas different," what are some creative ways you and your family could fund your giving?

4. Joe and Barb's grandchildren were greatly influenced by their trip to Haiti despite the discomforts of the third-world country. Where could you involve your children or grandchildren in seeing and practicing generosity?

CHAPTER TWENTY-ONE

Studying for the Final Exam

Robert E. Miller

H E WAS A businessman who never wore a tie. He hugged everyone, worked hard, attended Mass daily, and lived a recklessly generous life. Robert E. Miller desired to serve everyone God brought into his life, whether it was employees, waiters and waitresses, priests, or victims of tragedy.

After graduating from college and serving in the Korean War, Bob, as he was usually called, went to work for an insurance agency in Kansas City. In 1961, he struck out on his own and founded the Robert E. Miller Insurance Agency. Near the end of his life, Bob handed off the business to his two sons: Sean, chairman; and Matt, president. Today, the brothers manage the company based on principles and values they learned from their dad.

The Final Exam

In 1993, Bob was diagnosed with cancer and underwent surgery. During his recovery, an accident left Bob in the hospital with patches over his eyes.

"For five days, he was sitting there and could not do anything at all—which was very, very rare for our dad," Sean said. "After he came out of there, he said, 'I'm done; you guys run the company. I'm going to start working on the final exam.' He didn't think God would care too much about how good of an insurance man he was, but that God would want to know what he did to help other people."

Bob spent the rest of his life investing in God, his family, and others. Every day started with a prayer that God would send him someone he could help that day. "Every day he would be looking for that person he could help. It's a great way to live your life," Matt said. "Some days it was as simple as extra attention or a generous tip to a waiter."

Bob passed away on August 1, 2010, but his generous legacy lives on through his children, his grandchildren, and his business.

> "Every day started with a prayer that God would send him someone he could help that day."

Local and International Service

Helping other people was always a priority for Bob, and he committed himself to work both locally and internationally.

"Doing something a little bit odd and helping someone who wasn't being helped were his favorite things," Matt said. To name a few, Bob served with an organization helping refugees in Sudan, partnered with a group working with juvenile delinquents in Colorado, and hosted local and international priests and nuns in his home.

"He had a real love for the priesthood and religious life," Sean said. "He did a lot to help the sisters and the priests in the area."

"Bob organized an annual golf tournament to thank local priests for their service even though he was not a golfer himself. Also, Bob gave each priest a dress coat and shoes as a gift ... Which was another funny thing because our dad was probably the worst-dressed man in Kansas City," Sean laughed.

Today, Matt continues the golf tournament—which draws more than three hundred golfers—in his dad's honor. The event has grown into a nonprofit, C.O.R.E. (Celebrating Our Religion

Enthusiastically), that supports and thanks priests, seminarians, and consecrated religious workers.

Sean is responsible for another project of Bob's called "Homes from the Heart." Bob started Homes from the Heart after an earthquake in El Salvador in 2001. The organization has built over four hundred homes in El Salvador, Haiti, Nicaragua, and Guatemala. During the summer of 2011, Sean and his family traveled to El Salvador with the organization to build concrete houses. The trip was one way Sean has passed on a spirit of generosity to his four kids.

"We are trying to do things to make them realize it's not all about them," Sean said. "Dad was a great example of that. The trip to El Salvador was perfect because it was right in line with all of the stuff that he did. We started each day with Mass, worked hard all day, and enjoyed … dinner as a family."

Core Values

Bob didn't view money as something to cling to, but as a resource under his stewardship. His eagerness to give revealed what he valued most. "He usually found that other people needed the money more than he did, so he gave it away. He actually gave away so much that it made Mom nervous," Matt said. "He never got into fancy cars; he never got into any kind of self-indulgence. He just helped people out and got a big charge out of that."

Bob was also fervent about tithing personally and from his company's profit—a commitment Sean and Matt continue to uphold. "At the end of one year, he realized he hadn't tithed, so he went to the bank and borrowed money in order to make his tithe," Matt said. "The banker couldn't believe he was borrowing money to give it away, but he didn't care. His only concern was not letting a year close before he fulfilled his commitment to God."

Bob also helped implement a benevolence fund at the Miller Group to help employees (both former and current) and their families through hardships. The company matches every dollar employees donate, and a committee determines how to allocate the funds based on requests received from families in need.

"He took a very personal interest in helping each one of the folks with problems work their way out of them, whether it was through a loan or just advice that he gave," Sean said. Many times when someone requested help, he would tear up the request and personally help the individual.

> "The banker couldn't believe he was borrowing money to give it away ..."

Bob was not one to write down things or hash out detailed giving plans. He just lived his life as a model of generosity and hard work, and he expected his children to follow suit. Matt and Sean continue to run the Miller Group with a commitment to serve God and people, but perhaps in a more structured format than their father's spontaneous tendencies.

"We took all of his core values, the ones he had been pounding into our heads, and wrote them down," Matt said. "These core values are now printed on all our business cards. It is a good way to institutionalize Dad's good ideas and communicate them to the world."

Continuing a Legacy

Sean and Matt strongly believe their company is a platform for influencing people for God. Their work has created countless opportunities to support projects, individuals, and ministries. As they strive to be generous businessmen, they are learning to let God lead.

"If you slow down long enough to just listen to the people who are in your life on a daily basis, I think you get all the clues as to what you should be doing," Matt said.

The Miller brothers have experienced God's abundant blessings on their families and business, and they are grateful for the generous legacy of their father. They are continuing to model Bob's values in their own lives, always seeking to put God and people above their business. Although the business has performed well even through economic hardships, the boys still consider their greatest gift from their father to be the time he took to instill his values.

"I guess you might say we are studying for the final exam a little early," Matt said.

Although you may find Sean and Matt in suits and ties instead of mismatched clothing, and giving handshakes instead of hugs, you can be certain they are imitating the generosity instilled in them by Robert E. Miller.

Your Story:

1. Bob Miller's generous life left a legacy that greatly influenced his sons, their families, and their business. Think about your own biological or spiritual family. Who has left a legacy of generosity for you to imitate? What responsibility do you have to leave a legacy for the next generation?

2. Consider how you spend the majority of your time. Write out a typical day hour-by-hour. Which of these things are helping you study for the final exam? Have God and people become priorities in your life?

3. Talk to God and confess what competes for your attention. Ask Him to help you honor Him with your time and your resources.

Epilogue

A S YOU CONSIDER the stories in the preceding pages, there are certain themes that emerge. They are simple themes, but they require us to "own" them for ourselves. They can be summarized as follows:

1. God is the owner of everything I have.
2. I'm just a steward, a manager, of what God has given me.
3. I'm accountable for how I use the resources God has given me.
4. I want to use my resources to influence people's lives for eternity.

The process of how a person begins to personalize those themes can take a variety of paths:

1. A Bible study on stewardship with like-minded people
2. Obedience in giving at beginning levels
3. Trusting God to allow you to give beyond a tithe
4. A missions trip where your view of ministry gets a paradigm shift

5. Attending a Generous Giving Conference
6. Meeting with like-minded Christian advisors who can help you devise a giving plan
7. Seeing generosity being modeled by others

Whatever path your journey takes, rest assured it is one that takes you deeper into the heart of God. Indeed, God the Father gave up His most prized possession, His Son. Jesus gave up His heavenly position for a lowly, earthly tent. He gave up His life so that we might experience life.

But the end of that journey is a good one. No, it is a great one. This journey of generosity ends with joy. And that's a place I think we all want to be.

Looking to Jesus, the founder and perfecter of our faith, who for the joy that was set before him endured the cross, despising the shame, and is seated at the right hand of the throne of God. (Hebrews 12:2)

Generosity Resources

Acceptable Gift
www.acceptablegift.org
Acceptable Gift presents living and giving from God's perspec-
tive. Acceptable Gift offers books and resources that serve churches,
nonprofits, and individuals at all income and wealth levels.

Crown Financial Ministries
www.crown.org
Crown Financial Ministries equips servant leaders, churches, and
individuals to live by God's design for their finances, work, and life.

Generous Giving
www.generousgiving.org
Generous Giving provides generosity retreats, an annual event, and giver
stories to encourage people in their own generosity journey.

Halftime
www.halftime.org
Halftime works with mid-life marketplace leaders who desire to live the
second half of their lives rich in eternal significance.

iDonate

http://idonate.com

iDonate offers marketing support and helps ministries receive and process all donation types, including non-cash gifts.

Kingdom Advisors

http://kingdomadvisors.org

Kingdom Advisors is a community of Christian financial professionals integrating faith and practice for kingdom impact.

MAXIMUM Generosity—Brian Kluth

www.kluth.org

Brian Kluth provides resources, sermons, cartoons, and books on biblical stewardship, giving, tithing, and fundraising.

National Christian Foundation

www.nationalchristian.com

NCF is the largest Christian grant-making foundation in the world. They work with givers, ministries, and churches to create a culture of generosity.

About the Authors

William F. High is the Chief Executive Officer of National Christian Foundation *Heartland*. Formerly, he was a partner with the law firm Blackwell Sanders Peper Martin, LLP. He remains Of Counsel with Sanders Warren & Russell, LLP. He is also the founder of iDonate. com, BeFamily, and Generous Life. His aim is to change the paradigm by which people think about generosity and to make generosity generational.

William has been married to his wife, Brooke, for twenty-five years. They have four children: Ashley, Jessica, Nathan, and Joseph.

Missy Calvert is the editorial coordinator for *Sisterhood Magazine* at Premier Studios. She previously interned with Focus on the Family, Premier Studios, and the National Christian Foundation *Heartland*. She has a bachelor of arts in journalism and mass communications and a minor in English from Kansas State University. Missy desires to use the power of stories to connect people, inspire change, and ultimately bring God glory.

WinePressPublishing
Great Books, Defined.

To order additional copies of this book call:
1-877-421-READ (7323)
or please visit our website at
www.WinePressbooks.com

If you enjoyed this quality custom-published book,
drop by our website for more books and information.

www.winepresspublishing.com

"Your partner in custom publishing."